Java Regular Expressions: Taming the java.util.regex Engine

MEHRAN HABIBI

Java Regular Expressions: Taming the java.util.regex Engine
Copyright © 2004 by Mehran Habibi

ISBN (pbk): 1-59059-107-0

Printed and bound in the United States of America 12345678910

Trademarked names may appear in this book. Rather than use a trademark symbol with every occurrence of a trademarked name, we use the names only in an editorial fashion and to the benefit of the trademark owner, with no intention of infringement of the trademark.

Technical Reviewer: Bill Saez

Editorial Board: Steve Anglin, Dan Appleman, Gary Cornell, James Cox, Tony Davis, John Franklin, Chris Mills, Steven Rycroft, Dominic Shakeshaft, Julian Skinner, Jim Sumser, Karen Watterson, Gavin Wray, John Zukowski

Assistant Publisher: Grace Wong

Project Manager: Nate McFadden

Copy Editor: Nicole LeClerc

Production Manager: Kari Brooks

Production Editor: Laura Cheu

Proofreader: Linda Seifert

Compositor: Susan Glinert Stevens

Indexer: Kevin Broccoli

Artist: Kinetic Publishing Services, LLC

Cover Designer: Kurt Krames

Manufacturing Manager: Tom Debolski

Distributed to the book trade in the United States by Springer-Verlag New York, Inc., 175 Fifth Avenue, New York, NY, 10010 and outside the United States by Springer-Verlag GmbH & Co. KG, Tiergartenstr. 17, 69112 Heidelberg, Germany.

In the United States: phone 1-800-SPRINGER, email orders@springer-ny.com, or visit http://www.springer-ny.com. Outside the United States: fax +49 6221 345229, email orders@springer.de, or visit http://www.springer.de.

For information on translations, please contact Apress directly at 2560 Ninth Street, Suite 219, Berkeley, CA 94710. Phone 510-549-5930, fax 510-549-5939, email info@apress.com, or visit http://www.apress.com.

The source code for this book is available to readers at http://www.apress.com in the Downloads section. You will need to answer questions pertaining to this book in order to successfully download the code.

This book is dedicated to my lovely wife, Angela Young, MD.
I must have been really, really good in a previous life.

Contents at a Glance

Contents

About the Author

Mehran Habibi is the coauthor of *The Sun Certified Java Developer Exam with J2SE 1.4* (Apress, 2003) and *Cracking the AP Computer Science Exam, 2004-2005 Edition* (Princeton Review, 2004). He is also an application architect with BankOne in Ohio, where he resides with his lovely wife, Angela. Mehran has over nine years of IT experience, including positions with IBM, Executive Jet, UUNET, BankOne, and OCLC, in addition to working as a university lecturer, independent consultant, and Java certification trainer. Technologies of interest to him include Web services, wireless technologies, and XML/XSLT. Mehran's professional focus has been on architecture, project leadership, mentoring, team leadership, and programming from the mid-tier on back. Mehran holds certifications in both "The Other Company" and Java 2, and he graduated with a bachelor's of science degree in software engineering from the honors program at The Ohio State University.

Mehran is an amateur boxer, teaches martial arts at The Ohio State University, enjoys soccer, and has ruined his chess by playing too many speed games. You can contact him at coach@influxs.com.

About the Technical Reviewer

Bill Saez is a software engineer with Motorola in Ft. Lauderdale, Florida. While working with Motorola, Bill helped to create the world's first Java-powered wireless handset with J2ME and CLDC certification in 2000. Since then, he has continued to play an integral part in the commercialization and development of the J2ME platform and has authored several OEM APIs for iDEN handsets as well as J2ME Developer Guides for those products. Bill has been involved with Java development since its introduction and even served as a guinea pig for The Ohio State University's experimental Java software courses. He received his bachelor's degree in software engineering from The Ohio State University and is currently pursuing a master's degree in computer science from the University of Florida.

When he's not working or studying, Bill enjoys training for and running marathons, traveling with his family, and infrequently writing game reviews (http://www.epinions.com/user-billservo) in his copious spare time.

Acknowledgments

I'D LIKE TO THANK Nate McFadden, Gary Cornell, Nicole LeClerc, and Laura Cheu from Apress for being such a joy to work with. I'd also like to acknowledge the strong contributions of various friends, including Terry Camerlengo, the excellent people at JavaRanch (http://www.javaranch.com), and various kind others who provided feedback and suggestions. In particular, I'm grateful for Jim Yingst's fine critical eye. I would also like to acknowledge the strong mathematical analysis provided by my father, Dr. Javad Habibi. Last but certainly not least, I'd like to thank my technical reviewer, Bill Saez, for an amazing technical eye and a very gentle style. I can't wait to see your book there, Bill.

Introduction

THE FUNDAMENTAL GOAL of any computer language is the manipulation of data. Traditionally, Java has been an excellent language for doing so, provided that the data is represented as objects. However, Java's raw data manipulation mechanisms have always been somewhat lacking, especially when compared to the powerful machinations offered by languages such as Perl and awk.

The introduction of a standard regular expression package into Java 2 Standard Edition (J2SE) is an excellent step in rectifying this oversight. The `java.util.regex` package offers developers everything they need to use regular expressions in Java, all packaged in an easy-to-use, object-oriented structure. I think that you'll find that the `java.util.regex` package can become an extremely powerful tool in your programming arsenal, as well an elegant instrument that you'll enjoy using. After you've mastered it, you will wonder, as I did, how you ever managed without it.

What This Book Is About

This book is a comprehensive introduction to the regular expression support built into J2SE, and it's designed to help Java programmers who have little to no experience with regular expressions. It's meant to be both a reference and an explanatory text. Although a background in regular expressions is helpful, I don't make any such assumptions when presenting the material. The central aim is to help everyday programmers solve everyday problems.

After reading this text, you should be able to solve a great many of your routine text validation, searching, modification, and replacement problems quickly and efficiently by using Java's built-in regular expression support. Of course, this book also covers some advanced features of regular expressions. You should to be able to effectively use your new understanding of regular expressions as soon as you finish Chapter 1.

Who Should Read This Book

If you're new to regular expressions, but you're comfortable with the Java language, then this book is intended for you. If you have a background in regular expressions, but you need a reference for Java's regular expression package, you'll also find this book useful. However, if you're new to Java, you may find that you're better served by reading some introductory texts first. There are scores of good introductory books available, though my recommendations are *Head First Java* by Kathy Sierra and Bert Bates (O'Reilly & Associates, 2003) and *Thinking in Java, Third Edition* by Bruce Eckel (Prentice Hall, 2002). You can't go wrong with either book.

How This Book Is Structured

This book has five chapters and three appendixes. It's intended to be a progressive learning experience, so the chapters build on each other. I describe the contents of the chapters and appendixes in the following sections.

Chapter 1

This chapter introduces regular expressions and provides some simple examples and explanations to get you started. It explores the J2SE regular expression syntax, operations, and differences from regular expressions you might already be familiar with from other languages. It also offers a tutorial on regular expressions.

Even if you have a background in regular expressions, I suggest you look over the examples in this chapter—there are a lot of different regular expression flavors, and there's rarely an isomorphic mapping between them. Chapter 1 is a natural starting point if you're new to regular expressions in J2SE or if you need a refresher on regular expressions in general.

Chapter 2

Chapter 2 introduces the built-in Java support for regular expressions through the Pattern and Matcher classes. Each method and attribute is dissected in detail, and all but the most trivial have companion code examples that highlight appropriate usage. Chapter 2 covers which settings and flags might affect the efficiency of your code. Additionally, Chapter 2 details the five new methods on the String class that support regular expressions, and offers advice and examples regarding appropriate usage.

Chapter 3

Chapter 3 expounds on some advanced regular expression concepts, including groups, noncapturing groups, greedy qualifiers, positive qualifiers, reluctant qualifiers, possessive qualifiers, positive lookarounds, negative lookarounds, positive lookbehinds, and negative lookbehinds. It provides numerous examples and detailed explanations regarding how these concepts work and how they might benefit you in your day-to-day tasks.

Chapter 4

Chapter 4 offers advice and suggestions on using regular expressions in Java's object-oriented environment. The chapter covers best practices, examples, and lessons learned from similar packages.

Chapter 5

Chapter 5 provides numerous full-featured examples, with accompanying explanations and code, that build on the material presented in previous chapters. Chapter 5 is designed to illustrate the development process I use when I'm trying to solve a regular expression problem in Java.

Appendix A

Appendix A offers a complete listing, with explanation, of the regular expression syntax and various regular expression metacharacters.

Appendix B

Appendix B provides a summary of the methods of the `Pattern` and `Matcher` classes in Java.

Appendix C

Appendix C offers simple regular expressions, without accompanying code, to help with everyday, common tasks such as validating e-mails, checking text for format, extracting values, and so on.

CHAPTER 1

Regular Expressions

*"Everything, you see, makes sense, if you take
the trouble to work out the rational."*
— Piers Anthony

REGULAR EXPRESSIONS, or *regex* for short, describe text. They are a mechanism by which you can tell the Java Virtual Machine (JVM) how to find and potentially manipulate text for you. In this chapter, I'll examine and contrast the traditional approach of describing text with the regex approach.

For example, imagine you need to validate e-mail addresses. The verbal directions for doing so might be something along the lines of "Make sure the e-mail address contains an at (@) symbol." You could probably handle this task with a single line of Java code:

```
If (email.indexOf("@") > 0) {
    return true;
}
```

So far, so good. Suppose additional requirements creep in, though, as they invariably do. Now you also need to make sure that all e-mail addresses end with the .org extension. So you amend your code as follows:

```
If ((email.indexOf("@") > 0)  && ( email.endsWith(".org"))){

    return true;
}
```

But the requirements continue to creep. You now need all e-mail addresses to be of the form firstname_lastname, so you use the StringTokenizer to tokenize the e-mail address, extract the part before the @, look for the underscore (_) character, tokenize the strings around that, and so on. Pretty soon, you have some convoluted code for what should be a fairly straightforward operation.

The use of regular expressions can greatly simplify and condense this process. With regular expressions, you could write the following:

```
String regex = "[A-Za-z]+_[A-Za-z]+@[A-Za-z]+\\.org";
if (email.matches(regex)) return true;
```

In English, this means "Look for one or more letters, followed by an _, followed by one or more letters, followed by an @, followed by one or more letters, followed by .org." Notice that a period precedes the *o* in "org".

Don't be concerned if the syntax isn't completely clear to you right now—making it clear is the aim of this book. This chapter explores the underlying concepts of Java regex, with an emphasis on actually forming and using the regex syntax. It's a complete introduction to regular expressions, and it also serves as a preamble to the next chapter. Chapter 2, in turn, is a complete and exhaustive documentation of the J2SE regex object model.

The Building Blocks of Regular Expressions

Regular expressions in Java 2 Standard Edition (J2SE) consist of two essential parts, which are embodied by two new Java objects. The first part is a `Pattern`, and the second is a `Matcher`. Understanding these two objects is crucial to your ability to master regular expressions. Fortunately, they're easy concepts to understand.

I define these concepts in detail in the sections that follow, but at a general level, a *pattern* describes what you're searching for, and a *matcher* examines candidates that might match the pattern or description. For example, \s+ is a pattern describing one or spaces. Correspondingly, J2SE now provides the `Pattern` and `Matcher` objects.

> **NOTE**   When I refer to a candidate or a candidate string, I mean the string that the regex will be acting on. Thus, for the pattern described in the preceding section, a candidate string might be `coach@influxs.com`, `john_john_smith@w3c.org`, or `hana@saez.com`.

Defining Patterns

Patterns are the actual descriptions used in regular expressions. Their power stems from their capability to describe text, as opposed to specifying it. They're an important part of the regex vernacular, and you need to understand them well to use regular expressions. Fortunately, they're easy to grasp if you refuse to be intimidated, and their somewhat off-putting syntax soon becomes intuitive.

A pattern allows you to describe the characteristics of the item you're looking for, without specifying the item explicitly. This can be especially helpful when you only know the traits of your targets, but you're unable to name them specifically.

Imagine parsing a document. You might want to find every capitalized word; or every word beginning with the letter *Z*; or every word beginning with a capital *Z*, followed by a vowel, unless that vowel is an *a*. You can't know beforehand exactly what those words will be for a given document, but you can describe them. That description is your pattern.

I think of regular expressions as a police station. A pattern is the officer who takes a description of the suspects, and a matcher is the officer that rounds up and interrogates those suspects.

Defining Matchers

If you're familiar with Standard Query Language (SQL), it might help you to think of regular expressions as a sort of SQL for examining free-flowing text. A pattern is conceptually similar to the SQL query that's executed. A matcher corresponds to the ResultSet returned by that query.

A Matcher examines the results of applying a Pattern. If your pattern said, "Find every word starting with *a* in the previous sentence," then you would examine the Matcher after applying your pattern. Your code might look like Listing 1-1. The output for Listing 1-1 in shown in Output 1-1, which follows the listing.

Listing 1-1. Finding Every Occurrence of the Letter A

```java
import java.util.regex.*;

public class FindA{
  public static void main(String args[])
  throws Exception{

    String candidate =
     "A Matcher examines the results of applying a pattern.";

    //define the matching pattern as a
    //word boundary, a lowercase a, any
    //number of immediately trailing letters
    //numbers, or underscores, followed by
    //a word boundary
    String regex = "\\ba\\w*\\b";
    Pattern p = Pattern.compile(regex);

   //extract the Matcher for the String text
   Matcher m = p.matcher(candidate);
   String val=null;
```

```
    //display the original input string
    System.out.println("INPUT: " + candidate);

    //display the search pattern
    System.out.println("REGEX: " + regex +"\r\n");

  //examine the Matcher, and extract all
  //words starting with a lowercase a
    while (m.find())
    {
      val =  m.group();
      System.out.println("MATCH: " + val);
    }

    //if there were no matches, say so
    if (val == null) {
      System.out.println("NO MATCHES: ");
    }
  }
}
```

Output 1-1. Result of Running FindA

```
INPUT: A Matcher examines the results of applying a pattern.
REGEX: \ba\w*\b

MATCH: applying
MATCH: a
```

Again, it's not necessary that you be able to follow the code given in detail right now. I just want to establish a general sense of how things are done in J2SE regex. First, I define my Pattern:

```
Pattern p = Pattern.compile(regex);
```

Then, I feed my candidate string to the Pattern and extract a Matcher:

```
Matcher m = p.matcher(candidate);
```

Finally, I interrogate my Matcher:

```
while (m.find()) {....}
```

Creating Patterns

This section presents some simple techniques for writing your own regular expressions. I think of them as the *push,* the *pull,* and the *composition.* As in the Japanese martial art Judo, if your opponent is pushing against you, you pull him. If he's pulling away, you push. If those techniques don't work, you compose him into a pretzel.

Similarly, writing a regular expression will sometimes seem impervious to certain approaches, but very susceptible to others. The methods I describe in the following sections are only simple techniques for writing patterns. If you haven't already done so, you'll soon cultivate your own bag of regex tricks. You may even develop pet names for them.

The Pull Technique

One of the most successful ways to create regular expressions consists of taking an exact match and then slowly morphing it into a generic regular expression that matches the original. I think of this as the pull technique, because I'm slowly pulling the regular expression out of the exact match.

For example, imagine that you want to create a pattern to match four-digit numbers. Thus, *1234* would be a match, but *123* would not, and neither would *12345* or *ABCD.*

For the sake of this example, you'll need to introduce a single regular expression metacharacter, *\d,* that will match any digit ranging from *0* to *9.*

> **NOTE** A *metacharacter* describes another, more complex character. For example, *\n* is a metacharacter describing the nonprintable newline character.

Going back to the example, you know that

```
1234 matches 1234
```

This is, of course, obvious: Anything will match itself. However, you also know that \d matches any digit. By the transitive property of logic, you can substitute \d for the last digit. Thus, the pattern becomes

```
1234 should_match 123\d
```

Here you replace the last digit, *4*, with the equivalent metacharacter, *\d*. If you run this pattern though the handy RX.java program, you can see that it does, in fact, continue to match. So far, so good. Actually, it's better than good: Now you have a pattern that will match not only *1234*, but also any four-digit number beginning with the digits *123*. We're getting closer.

> **NOTE** RX.java is a very short companion program for this book that you can obtain from Downloads section of the Apress Web site (http://www.apress.com). You can use this program to execute regular expression patterns against a candidate string.

Repeat the process on the third digit, so that *1234* should match *12\d\d*, where you replace the *3* with the equivalent *\d*. Things are looking up. Not only does this match *1234*, but also it matches any four-digit number beginning with the digits *12*.

You can see where this is going. Eventually, you'll create the pattern *\d\d\d\d*, which will match any four digits. This isn't the most succinct pattern, but it's sufficient to meet the stated need: It matches any four-digit number.

The point here is that you can, in principle, sometimes work *backward* from a specific match to create the pattern you need. Of course, this is just a technique, and it won't work for all situations. However, it's a good method to put into your regex bag of tricks.

The Push Technique

Another technique that I've found to be helpful in writing regular expression patterns is the push technique. The push technique builds on previous work by either adding to it, subtracting from it, or modifying its scope until it's useful.

Instead of working with a specific matching token, as in the pull technique, this approach takes a preexisting regular expression that's similar to the one you need and modifies it until it does the required job. That is, the regular expression is pushed into another functionality, hence the name.

For example, say you want a regex pattern that matches five digits. Based on the previous example, you know that *\d\d\d\d* will match any four digits. Thus, the process of finding a match for a five-digit match is as easy as appending another *\d* to the previous pattern. The answer, of course, is the pattern *\d\d\d\d\d*.

As you progress though this chapter, you'll learn that these aren't the most elegant representations of the four-digit and five-digit matching patterns you could come up with, but they're perfectly legitimate solutions, and they're reasonably derived. That process of derivation is the important point to take away from this discussion.

The Composition Technique

The composition technique does exactly what its name implies: It puts together various patterns to form a new whole. That is, it's the composition of a new pattern by using other patterns. This is distinct from the push technique in that patterns aren't modified; rather, they're simply appended.

Assume that you need to create a pattern that will match United States zip codes, which consist of five digits, followed by a hyphen character, followed by four digits. Based on the work you've already done, this pattern is very easy to create. You know that four digits match $\textit{\textbackslash d\textbackslash d\textbackslash d\textbackslash d}$, that a hyphen matches itself, and that five digits match $\textit{\textbackslash d\textbackslash d\textbackslash d\textbackslash d\textbackslash d}$. Composing these into a single pattern yields the pattern $\textit{\textbackslash d\textbackslash d\textbackslash d\textbackslash d\textbackslash d-\textbackslash d\textbackslash d\textbackslash d\textbackslash d}$.

Again, this isn't the most elegant and concise representation for a zip code, and it isn't very permissive (what about five-digit zip codes? What if there are spaces between the hyphen and the digits? What if there is no hyphen, just a space?), but it does meet the stated requirement.

> **NOTE** As with most software problems, you can often find the solution to a regex conundrum by clarifying the requirements.

Introducing the Regular Expression Syntax

The following sections introduce Java's regular expression syntax. For the sake of clarity, the material is grouped into small, logical units, followed by a brief example that demonstrates usage. The examples progress from those that emphasize the role of the Pattern to those that start to rely on the Matcher more.

> **NOTE** Please keep in mind that these are working examples only. We're not ready to bulletproof our code yet.

Reading Patterns

The regcx language contains metacharacters designed to help you describe search criteria. Because reading a pattern without being aware of these characters can be a bewildering experience, I've listed the most popular metacharacters are in Table 1-1.

These characters are effectively reserved words, just as new is a reserved word in Java. They serve as building blocks for more complex search criteria. I discuss this in more detail soon.

Table 1-1. Basic Regex Delimiter Characters

Pattern	Name	Description
.	Period	Matches any character.
$	Dollar sign	Matches the end of a line.
^	Carat	Matches the beginning of a line.
{	Opening curly bracket	Defines a range opening.
[	Opening bracket	Defines a character class opening.
(	Opening parenthesis	Defines the beginning of a group.
|	Pipe symbol	A symbol meaning OR
}	Closing curly bracket	Defines a range closing.
]	Closing bracket	Defines a character class closing.
)	Closing parenthesis	Defines the closing of a group.
*	Asterisk	The preceding is repeated zero or more times.
+	Plus sign	The preceding is repeated one or more times.
?	Question mark	The preceding is repeated zero or one time.
\	Backward slash	The following is not to be treated as a metacharacter.

If you're reading a character in a regex pattern and it isn't one of characters listed in Table 1-1, then the character you're reading probably stands for the character it represents. For example, Table 1-2 shows how the pattern *hello** should be read.

Table 1-2. The Pattern **hello***

Letter	Description
h	The character *h*
e	Followed by the character *e*
l	Followed by the character *l*
l	Followed by the character *l*
o	Followed by the character *o*
*	Followed by a metacharacter that, in this case, means *o* should be repeated zero or more times

* **In English:** Look for the word *hell*, followed by any number of trailing *o* characters.

If you actually need to find one of these characters, such as the * character, simply append the character you're searching for to a \ character. For example, to find the * character, use *.

Common and Boundary Characters

Regular expressions also contain characters that take on special meaning when they're delimited by the \ character. These facilitate finding common tokens, such as word boundaries, empty spaces, tabs, alphanumeric characters, and so on. For example, *n* and *t* are special characters that represent a newline and a tab, respectively.

In this section, I cover these common boundary characters and provide examples of their use.

Common Characters

Certain types of characters occur often enough that regular expression languages have developed a shorthand for referring to them. For example, a digit is designated by the *d* expression. Without the \ character delimiting the *d*, the expression would simply refer to the fourth letter of the English alphabet, in lowercase. Table 1-3 lists some of these common characters.

Table 1-3. Common and Boundary Characters

Character	Description
.	Matches any character; may also match line terminators.
\d	A digit *[0-9]*. This will match any single digit from *0* to *9*. Notice that an input of *19* will need to match twice: Once for the *1* and once again for the *9*.
\D	A nondigit *[^0-9]*. This will match any character that isn't a digit, including a whitespace character.
\w	A word character *[a-zA-Z_0-9]*. This will match any character from *a* to *z* or *A* to *Z*, an underscore, or any single digit from *0* to *9*.
\W	A nonword character *[^\w]*. This will match any character that isn't a word character, such as a number, including whitespace characters.
\t	The tab character.
\n	The newline (linefeed) character.
\r	The carriage-return character.
\f	The form-feed character.
\s	A whitespace character. This includes the newline, carriage-return, tab, form-feed, and end-of-line characters.
\S	A non-whitespace character, also known as *[^\s]*. This will match any character that isn't a whitespace character, as described previously.
^	The beginning of a line.
$	The end of a line.
\b	A word boundary. A *word boundary* is the character immediately preceding what we think of as "words" in English vernacular, corresponding to *\w* previously. It will also match the character immediately following a word. Most often, this character matches a space, a tab, an end of a line, or a beginning of a line.
\B	A non–word boundary.

Common Characters Example

Imagine that you need to verify that a given String consists of any alphanumeric character, including underscores, followed by a digit. Thus, you would accept *A1*, but not *!1*, because the *!* symbol isn't an alphanumeric character or an underscore. The pattern you want in this case consists of an alphanumeric character (or underscore) followed by a digit; thus, *\w\d*, per Table 1-1.

The pattern *\w\d* will match *h1*, *k9*, *A1*, or *l1*, because each consists of an alphanumeric character followed by a digit. It won't match *AA*, *9A*, or **5*, because these don't consist of an alphanumeric character followed by a digit. Table 1-4 dissects the pattern.

Table 1-4. The Pattern \w\d

Regex	Description
\w	Any character ranging from *a* to *z*, *A* to *Z*, *0* to *9*, or an underscore
\d	Followed by a single digit ranging from *0* to *9*

* **In English:** Look for any alphanumeric character, or the underscore character, followed by a single digit.

Boundary Characters

Regular expressions also provide a mechanism for finding common character boundaries. These include newlines, end-of-line characters, end-of-file characters, tabs, and so on. These are listed in the latter part of Table 1-3.

Boundary Characters Example

Say you want to match the word *anna* from an input string, but only if it's at the beginning of a word. Thus, *Hanna* wouldn't fit your criteria. The pattern you want in this case consists of a word boundary, *\b*, followed by the characters *a*, *n*, *n*, and *a*, thus the regex *\banna*.

The pattern ***banna** will match *anna* but not *Hanna*, because *anna* is a cluster of characters preceded by a space character. A space character meets the criterion of being a word boundary. This isn't true of *Hanna*, because the character immediately preceding the *a* character in *Hanna* is an *H*, and *H* isn't a word boundary. Table 1-5 dissects the pattern.

Table 1-5. The Pattern **banna**

Regex	Description
\b	A word boundary
a	Followed by the character *a*
n	Followed by the character *n*
n	Followed by the character *n*
a	Followed by the character *a*

* **In English:** Look for *anna* if it is the beginning of a word.

Quantifiers and Alternates

Quantifiers and *alternates* allow you to specify the number of tokens you need to find or alternative tokens you're willing to accept. Table 1-6 lists some of the quantifiers and alternates in regex.

Table 1-6. Quantifiers

Regex	Description
?	The preceding is repeated once or not at all.
*	The preceding is repeated zero or more times.
+	The preceding is repeated one or more times.
{n}	The preceding is repeated exactly *n* times.
{n,}	The preceding is repeated at least *n* times.
{n,m}	The preceding is repeated at least *n* times, but no more than *m* times. This includes *m* repetitions.
|	The element preceding the | or the element following it.

The following sections offer some examples that demonstrate working with quantifiers.

Repeated Characters Example 1

The pattern *An+a* will match *Ana, Anna,* or *Annnna* because each contains at least one *A* character immediately followed by one or more *n* characters followed by an *a* character. It won't match *Aa* or *ANna* because these don't consist of a single *A* character immediately followed by at least one *n* character followed by an *a* character. Notice that a capital *N* and a lowercase *n* aren't considered matches. Table 1-7 dissects the pattern.

Table 1-7. The Pattern An+a

Regex	Description
A	The character *A*
n+	Followed by one or more *n* characters
a	Followed by the character *a*

* **In English:** Look for a capital *A*, followed by one or more *n* characters, followed by an *a* character.

There is some interesting behavior that can be elicited here. If this match had been performed using the String.matches method, the pattern would not have matched *AnnaMarie*, because the String.matches method requires an exact match, and the *Marie* part of *AnnaMarie* would have ruined that exactness. However, the Matcher.find method would have matched *AnnaMarie* because it's more permissive. Stay tuned—more details coming soon.

Repeated Characters Example 2

The pattern *A{2,7}* will match *AA, AAAA,* or *AAAAAAA* because each of these contains at least at least two *A* characters and no more than seven *A* characters. The pattern won't match *A* because it contains less than two *A* characters, and the pattern won't match *AAAAAAAA* because it contains more than seven *A* characters. Table 1-8 dissects the pattern.

Table 1-8. The Pattern A{2,7}

Regex	Description
A	The character *A*
{	Open repeating group
2	Repeated at least two times
,	But not more than
7	Seven times
}	Close repeated group

* **In English:** Look for a sequence of the character *A* repeated two, three, four, five, six, or seven times.

> **NOTE**   In the example at the beginning of this chapter, you needed a pattern to match four consecutive digits and derived *\d\d\d\d*. As noted, this isn't the most elegant pattern possible. An alternative, yet equivalent, way of expressing the same pattern is *\d{4}*, per Table 1-6—that is, a sequence of exactly four digits.

Alternative Characters Example 1

The pattern *A|B* will match *A* or *B*, because each consists of either an *A* character or a *B* character. It won't match *P*, *Q*, or *jelly* because these don't consist strictly of either an *A* or a *B* character. Table 1-9 dissects this pattern.

Table 1-9. The Pattern A|B

Regex	Description
A	The character *A*
|	Or
B	The character *B*

* **In English:** Look for either a capital *A* or a capital *B*.

Alternative Characters Example 2

The pattern ***anna|marie*** will match *anna* or *marie*, because *anna* matches the first alternative and *marie* matches the second. It won't match *Josie, Ralph*, or *Doctor*. Table 1-10 dissects the pattern.

Table 1-10. The Pattern **anna|marie**

Regex	Description
anna	The characters *a, n, n,* and *a,* in order
|	Or
marie	The characters *m, a, r, i,* and *e,* in order

* **In English:** Look for either the word *anna* or the word *marie*.

So would the pattern match *annamarie* as a single word? In a word, maybe. I provide detailed information about this topic in later chapters, but here's the nickel tour. Java 2 Enterprise Edition's (J2EE's) regex allows you to specify whether you need an exact or partial match. Thus, *annamarie* would match the pattern ***anna|marie*** twice for a partial match, and not at all for an exact match. Without going into too much detail, `String.matches` only provides for exact matches, whereas the `Matcher` class can provide more lenient matches using the `find` method.

What about the pattern ***Miss anna|marie***? Will it match *Miss marie* and *Miss anna*, or just one of them? Or will it match neither? A strict match will match *Miss anna* but reject *Miss marie*. The alternative | will read *Miss anna* as a single option and the pattern *marie* as another. Because the pattern ***maria*** isn't equal to the candidate *Miss maria*, the search will reject *Miss maria*.

Character Classes

There are times when you need to describe your search criteria as a *class*—that is, as a group that shares potentially complex commonalities that you need to be able to describe and for which there are no predefined classes. Fortunately, regex provides a mechanism for doing so through character classes, as shown in Table 1-11.

Table 1-11. Character Classes

Pattern	Description
[abc]	*a*, *b*, or *c*. (Of course, any character could be used, not just *a*, *b*, or *c*.)
[^abc]	Any character except *a*, *b*, or *c*.
[a-zA-Z]	*a* through *z* or *A* through *Z*.
[a-d[m-p]]	*a* through *d*, or *m* through *p*: *[a-dm-p]*.
[a-z&&[def]]	Whatever exists in both sets, namely *d*, *e*, or *f*.
[a-z&&[^bc]]	*a* through *z*, except for *b* and *c*: *[ad-z]*.
[a-z&&[^m-p]]	*a* through *z*, and not *m* through *p*: *[a-lq-z]*.

There are also some predefined Portable Operating System Interface for UNIX (POSIX) character classes. These are American Standard Code for Information Interchange (ASCII) classes that experience has shown to be particularly useful. Thus, they're already in place, and you can simply refer to them for use. Table 1-12 contains the POSIX character classes.

Table 1-12. POSIX Character Classes

Pattern	Description
\p{Lower}	A lowercase letter: *[a-z]*
\p{Upper}	An uppercase letter: *[A-Z]*
\p{ASCII}	All ASCII characters: *[\x00-\x7F]*
\p{Alpha}	An upper- or lowercase letter: *[\p{Lower}\p{Upper}]*
\p{Digit}	A digit: *[0-9]*
\p{Alnum}	A number or a letter: *[\p{Alpha}\p{Digit}]*
\p{Punct}	Punctuation: one of *!"#$%&'()*+,-./:;<=>?@[\]^_`{|}~*
\p{Graph}	Any visible character: *[\p{Alnum}\p{Punct}]*
\p{Print}	A printable character: *[\p{Graph}]*
\p{Blank}	A tab or space
\p{Cntrl}	A control character: *[\x00-\x1F\x7F]*
\p{XDigit}	A hexadecimal digit: *[0-9a-fA-F]*
\p{Space}	A whitespace character: *[\t\n\x0B\f\r]*

Simple Class Example

Let's step through some simple examples. The pattern *[0-5]* will match any part of the input that contains a digit between *0* and *5*. Thus, it will match on *0*, *1*, *2*, *3*, *4*, or *5*. It won't match *8*, *6*, or any nondigit characters. Table 1-13 dissects the pattern.

Table 1-13. The Pattern [0-5]

Regex	Description
[	A class consisting of
0	The digit 0
-	Ranging through
5	The digit 5
]	Close class

* **In English:** Look for any digit ranging from *0* to *5*, including *0* and *5*.

Negation Example

The pattern *[^A]* will match any character except the character *A*. This includes other characters, spaces, tabs, punctuation, and so on. It's important to notice that the ^ delimiter only has a not meaning when inside a class bracket—that is, inside the *[* and *]* brackets. Outside those brackets, it stands for the beginning of the line character. I cover this topic in more detail later. Table 1-14 dissects the pattern.

Table 1-14. The Pattern [^A]

Regex	Description
[	A class consisting of
^	Any character except
A	The character *A*
]	Close class

* **In English:** Look for any character except the capital letter *A*.

Groups and Back References

Groups are simply logical divisions of the text. When you describe a group in regex, you're providing a mechanism for the JVM to treat characters that fall into that group in a specific way.

Back references allow the regex pattern to refer to a group, even as it's in the middle of an operation. A pattern can refer to the last group it found, or the one before that, or even one further down the execution chain.

In the sections that follow, I cover the topics of groups and back references in more detail and present an example for each.

Groups

A group is a submatch. If you're familiar with SQL, it might be helpful to think of groups as the SQL equivalent of a subquery. Groups allow you to define parts of your pattern as logical subunits of the whole and then refer to the results of those subunits. Their syntax follows in Table 1-15.

Table 1-15. Groups

Regex	Description
(	A group consisting of
...	Any regex pattern
)	Close group

Groups Example

As with most things, an example can be more illuminating than a description. Consider the pattern *(\w+)_(\w+)@(\w+)\.org* to match e-mail patterns. Table 1-16 dissects this pattern.

Table 1-16. The Pattern (\w+)_(\w+)@(\w+)\.org

Regex	Description
(	A group consisting of
\w	An alphanumeric or underscore character
+	Repeated one or more times
)	Close group
_	Followed by an underscore character
(	A group consisting of
\w	One alphanumeric or underscore character
+	Followed by one or more alphanumeric characters
)	Close group
@	Followed by an at character
(	A group consisting of
\w	One alphanumeric or underscore character
+	Followed by one or more alphanumeric or underscore characters
)	Close group
\.	Followed by the period character
o	Followed by the character *o*
r	Followed by the character *r*
g	Followed by the character *g*

* **In English:** Look for a group of alphanumeric characters, followed by _, followed by a group of alphanumeric characters, followed by @, followed by a group of alphanumeric characters, followed by *.org*.

Back References

Back references are one of the most powerful features offered by regular expressions. Unfortunately, programmers often skip over them because they're not explained well in the regular expression literature. That's a mistake I hope to rectify here.

Back references allow a pattern to refer back to parts of itself. They always refer back to groups that were enclosed by the "*(*" and the "*)*" characters. Table 1-17 presents the syntax for back references.

Table 1-17. Back References

Regex	Description
\1	The first group in the pattern
\2	The second group in the pattern
\n	The *n*th group in the pattern

> **NOTE** There are some idiosyncratic behaviors associated with how back references work in Java, which I explain later in this chapter and in Chapter 3. For right now, you have enough information on back references to get started.

Back References Example

Say you need to find matches in which a word is duplicated. That is, you don't know what the word you're looking for is, but you want to be alerted when the same word is repeated twice in a row. If you've used a word processor such as Microsoft Word, you'll notice that the application does this automatically. Let's explore how you might do this in Java.

You'll use the pattern *\b(\w+) \1\b*, which is dissected in Table 1-18. This pattern matches *pizza pizza*, *Faster pussycat kill kill*, or *Never Never Never Never Never* because each contains a word that's immediately repeated. It won't match *222 2222*, *sara sarah*, or *Faster pussycat kill, kill* because these don't contain a word that's immediately repeated. The latter group won't match because *222 2222* has a lingering *2* in the second set, *sara sarah* has a lingering *h* in the second word, and in *Faster pussycat kill, kill* the second *kill* is separated from the first by a comma.

Table 1-18. The Pattern \b(\w+) \1\b

Regex	Description
\b	A word boundary
(	Followed by a group consisting of
\w	Any alphanumeric character
+	Repeated one for more times
)	Close group
<space>	Followed by a space
\1	Followed by the exact group of characters captured previously
\b	Followed by a word boundary

---

* **In English:** Look for a word boundary, followed by a group of alphanumeric characters, followed by a space, followed by the *exact same group of alphanumeric characters found previously,* followed by a word boundary. In short, look for duplicate words.

In the next section, you'll examine some practical examples with corresponding Java code.

Integrating Java with Regular Expressions

Thus far, you've worked almost exclusively with regular expressions, but not really with Java. Now it's time to consider how the two interact. The following examples differ from the preceding ones in that they incorporate Java code with regular expressions. They offer a more complete picture of how you can use some J2SE regex syntax.

Some of the regular expressions you'll see here are slightly more advanced than in the examples you've seen previously, as they build on the fundamentals discussed thus far in the chapter. For example, Listing 1-2 combines groups with quantifiers.

Don't be discouraged if the patterns themselves aren't completely clear to you right now. An intuitive understanding will develop as you continue to read this book. Focus on the concepts and become comfortable with how the Java code and the regex complement each other.

There are only two pieces of information you need to take full advantage of the following examples:

- Any \-delimited regex expression metacharacter needs to be delimited once again when it's used in Java code. Thus, *\d* becomes *\\d* and *\s* becomes *\\s* in your Java code. Correspondingly, a more complex expression such as *(\d-)?(\d{3}-)?\d{3}-\d{4}\s* becomes *(\\d-)?(\\d{3}-)?\\d{3}-\\d{4}\\s* in Java code. All \ characters are doubled to produce \\ when they're used in a String object.

- In this book, when I talk about a regular expression in and of itself, I don't use the double delimiting mechanism. However, I do when working with specific coding examples.

- The String.matches(String regex) method is a new method that has been added to the String class. It compares the String it's called on to the given regular expression, regex, and returns true if the regex pattern matches the String *exactly*. To match exactly means that the String in question can't contain any characters—not even invisible characters such as newlines and spaces—that aren't accounted for in the regex pattern.

Confirming Phone Number Formats Example

The code in Listing 1-2 simply determines if the given phone number meets the criteria of being well formatted. It takes advantage of two metacharacters introduced in Table 1-6. Specifically it uses range, *{n,m}*, indicating that the previous character or class must be repeated at least *n* times and no more than *m* times. It also uses the *?* character, indicating the previous character or class must be present zero or one time.

The pattern as a whole checks for seven digits preceded by optional country and area codes. Output 1-2 shows the result of running the program, and Table 1-19 dissects the pattern.

Listing 1-2. MatchPhoneNumber.java

```
import java.util.regex.*;
public class MatchPhoneNumber{
    public static void main(String args[]){
        isPhoneValid(args[0]);
    }

    /**
    * Confirms that the format for the given phone number is valid.
    * @param phone is a String representing the phone number.
    * @returns true if the phone number format is acceptable.
    */
```

```
public static boolean isPhoneValid(String phone){
   boolean retval=false;

   String phoneNumberPattern =
     "(\\d-)?(\\d{3}-)?\\d{3}-\\d{4}";

   retval= phone.matches(phoneNumberPattern);

   //prepare a message indicating success or failure       -
   String msg = "   NO MATCH: pattern:" + phone
           + "\r\n            regex: " + phoneNumberPattern;

   if (retval){
   msg = "   MATCH   : pattern:" + phone
        + "\r\n            regex: " + phoneNumberPattern;
   }

   System.out.println(msg +"\r\n");
   return retval;
 }
}
```

Output 1-2. Result of Running MatchPhoneNumber.java

```
C:\RegEx\Examples\chapter1>java MatchPhoneNumber "1-999-111-2222"
   MATCH   : pattern:1-999-111-2222
            regex: (\d-)?(\d{3}-)?\d{3}-\d{4}


C:\RegEx\Examples\chapter1>java MatchPhoneNumber "999-111-2222"
   MATCH   : pattern:999-111-2222
            regex: (\d-)?(\d{3}-)?\d{3}-\d{4}

C:\RegEx\Examples\chapter1>java MatchPhoneNumber "1-111-2222"
   MATCH   : pattern:1-111-2222
            regex: (\d-)?(\d{3}-)?\d{3}-\d{4}

C:\RegEx\Examples\chapter1>java MatchPhoneNumber "111-2222"
   MATCH   : pattern:111-2222
            regex: (\d-)?(\d{3}-)?\d{3}-\d{4}
```

```
C:\RegEx\Examples\chapter1>java MatchPhoneNumber "1.999-111-2222"
    NO MATCH: pattern:1.999-111-2222
              regex: (\d-)?(\d{3}-)?\d{3}-\d{4}


C:\RegEx\Examples\chapter1>java MatchPhoneNumber "999 111-2222"
    NO MATCH: pattern:999 111-2222
              regex: (\d-)?(\d{3}-)?\d{3}-\d{4}


C:\RegEx\Examples\chapter1>java MatchPhoneNumber "1 111 2222"
    NO MATCH: pattern:1 111 2222
              regex: (\d-)?(\d{3}-)?\d{3}-\d{4}


C:\RegEx\Examples\chapter1>java MatchPhoneNumber "111-JAVA"
    NO MATCH: pattern:111-JAVA
              regex: (\d-)?(\d{3}-)?\d{3}-\d{4}
```

Table 1-19. The Pattern (\d-)?(\d{3}-)?\d{3}-\d{4}

Regex	Description
(	A group consisting of
\d	A digit
-	Followed by a hyphen (-)
)	The end of this group
?	Look for zero or one of the preceding
(	Followed by a group consisting of
\d	A digit
{	Repeated at least
3	Three times
}	End repetition
-	Followed by a hyphen
)	The end of this group
?	Look for zero or one of the preceding
\d	Followed by a digit
{	Repeated at least

Table 1-19. The Pattern (\d-)?(\d{3}-)?\d{3}-\d{4} (Continued)

Regex	Description
3	Three times
}	End repetition
-	Followed by a hyphen
\d	Followed by a digit
{	Repeated at least
4	Four times
}	End repetition

* **In English:** Look for a single digit followed by a hyphen. This is optional. Then, look for three digits followed by a hyphen. This is also optional. Next, look for three digits, followed by a hyphen, followed by four digits.

Confirming Zip Codes Example

The code in Listing 1-3 determines if the zip code meets the criterion of being well formatted. It checks for five digits optionally followed by a hyphen and four digits. Output 1-3 shows the result of running the program. Table 1-20 dissects the pattern.

Listing 1-3. MatchZipCodes.java

```
import java.util.regex.*;
import java.io.*;

public class MatchZipCodes{
   public static void main(String args[]){
      isZipValid(args[0]);
   }

   /**
   * Confirms that the format for the given zip code is valid.
   * @param zip is a String representing the zip code.
   * @returns true if the zip code format is acceptable.
   */
   public static boolean isZipValid(String zip){
      boolean retval=false;
```

```
        String zipCodePattern = "\\d{5}(-\\d{4})?";
        retval = zip.matches(zipCodePattern);

        //prepare a message indicating success or failure
        String msg = "   NO MATCH: pattern:" + zip
              + "\r\n                regex: " + zipCodePattern;

        if (retval){
        msg = "   MATCH    : pattern:" + zip
            + "\r\n                regex: " + zipCodePattern;
        }

        System.out.println(msg +"\r\n");
        return retval;
    }
}
```

Output 1-3. Result of Running MatchZipCodes.java

```
C:\RegEx\Examples\chapter1>java MatchZipCodes "45643-4443"
   MATCH    : pattern:45643-4443
             regex: \d{5}(-\d{4})?

C:\RegEx\Examples\chapter1>java MatchZipCodes "45643"
   MATCH    : pattern:45643
             regex: \d{5}(-\d{4})?

C:\RegEx\Examples\chapter1>java MatchZipCodes "443"
   NO MATCH: pattern:443
             regex: \d{5}(-\d{4})?

C:\RegEx\Examples\chapter1>java MatchZipCodes "45643-44435"
   NO MATCH: pattern:45643-44435
             regex: \d{5}(-\d{4})?

C:\RegEx\Examples\chapter1>java MatchZipCodes "45643 44435"
   NO MATCH: pattern:45643 44435
             regex: \d{5}(-\d{4})?
```

Table 1-20. The Pattern \d{5}(-\d{4})?

Regex	Description
\d	A digit
{	Repeated at least
5	Five times
}	End repetition
(	Open group
-	Consisting of a hyphen
\d	A digit
{	Repeated at least
4	Four times
}	End repetition
)	The end of this group
?	Look for zero or one of the preceding

* **In English:** Look for five digits, optionally followed by a hyphen and four digits.

Confirming Dates Example

The code in Listing 1-4 checks the format of a given date. It confirms that given date format consists of one or two digits followed by a hyphen, followed by one or two digits, followed by a hyphen, followed by four digits. Output 1-4 shows the result of running the program. Table 1-21 dissects the pattern.

Listing 1-4. MatchDates.java

```java
import java.util.regex.*;
import java.io.*;

public class MatchDates{
   public static void main(String args[]){
      isDateValid(args[0]);
   }
```

```
/**
 * Confirms that given date format consists of one or two digits
 * followed by a hyphen, followed by one or two digits, followed
 * by a hyphen, followed by four digits
 * @param date is a String representing the date.
 * @returns true if date format is acceptable.
 */
public static boolean isDateValid(String date){
    boolean retval=false;

    String datePattern ="\\d{1,2}-\\d{1,2}-\\d{4}";
    retval = date.matches(datePattern);

    //prepare a message indicating success or failure
    String msg = "   NO MATCH: pattern:" + date
            + "\r\n                regexLength: " + datePattern;

    if (retval){
    msg = "   MATCH   : pattern:" + date
        + "\r\n                regexLength: " + datePattern;
    }

    System.out.println(msg +"\r\n");
    return retval;
  }
}
```

Output 1-4. Result of Running MatchDates.java

```
C:\RegEx\Examples\chapter1>java MatchDates "04-02-1999"
   MATCH   : pattern:04-02-1999
            regexLength: \d{1,2}-\d{1,2}-\d{4}


C:\RegEx\Examples\chapter1>java MatchDates "15-42-1999"
   MATCH   : pattern:15-42-1999
            regexLength: \d{1,2}-\d{1,2}-\d{4}


C:\RegEx\Examples\chapter1>java MatchDates "April fourth nineteen ninety nine"
   NO MATCH: pattern:April fourth nineteen ninety nine
            regexLength: \d{1,2}-\d{1,2}-\d{4}
```

```
C:\RegEx\Examples\chapter1>java MatchDates "15-42-20002"
   NO MATCH: pattern:15-42-20002
              regexLength: \d{1,2}-\d{1,2}-\d{4}


C:\RegEx\Examples\chapter1>java MatchDates "02-02-20002"
   NO MATCH: pattern:02-02-20002
              regexLength: \d{1,2}-\d{1,2}-\d{4}


C:\RegEx\Examples\chapter1>java MatchDates "04-02-02"
   NO MATCH: pattern:04-02-02
              regexLength: \d{1,2}-\d{1,2}-\d{4}



C:\RegEx\Examples\chapter1>java MatchDates "04-02-garbage"
   NO MATCH: pattern:04-02-garbage
              regexLength: \d{1,2}-\d{1,2}-\d{4}
```

Table 1-21. The Pattern \d{1,2}-\d{1,2}-\d{4}

Regex	Description
\d	A digit
{	Repeated at least
1	One time
,	But no more than
2	Two times
}	Close repetition
-	Followed by a hyphen
\d	Followed by a digit
{	Repeated at least
1	One time
,	But no more than
2	Two times
}	Close repetition
-	Followed by a hyphen

Table 1-21. The Pattern \d{1,2}-\d{1,2}-\d{4} (Continued)

Regex	Description
\d	Followed by a digit
{	Repeated at least
1	Four times
}	Close repetition

* **In English:** Look for one or two digits, followed by a hyphen, followed by one or two digits, followed by a hyphen, followed by four digits.

Confirming Name Formats Example

The code in Listing 1-5 determines if the given name meets the criterion of being well formatted. It looks for a first name token, an optional middle name token, and finally a last name token. For this example's purposes, a name token consists of a capital letter followed by any number of lowercase letters.

This example is interesting because it takes advantage of Java's robustness to a degree that the previous example didn't. Specifically, you define what you mean when you say a "name token":

```
String nameToken ="\\p{Upper}(\\p{Lower}+\\s?)";
```

Then you use that definition later:

```
String namePattern = "("+nameToken+"){2,3}";
```

> **NOTE** *\p{Upper}* and *\p{Lower}* are described shortly. They simply mean any uppercase character and any lowercase character, respectively.

This helps to keep the regex pattern from becoming overwhelming, and it also helps to isolate errors. As the examples in this book grow more ambitious, you'll start to see that coupling regular expressions with Java's powerful language can offer benefits that would, at best, be terse using regular expressions alone. Listing 1-5 shows the program `MatchNameFormats.java`, Output 1-5 shows the result of running the program, and Table 1-22 dissects the pattern.

Listing 1-5. MatchNameFormats.java

```java
import Java.util.regex.*;
import java.io.*;

public class MatchNameFormats{
    public static void main(String args[]){

        isNameValid(args[0]);
    }

    /**
     * Confirms that the format for the given name is valid.
     * @param name is a String representing the name.
     * @returns true if the name format is acceptable.
     */
    public static boolean isNameValid(String name){
      boolean retval=false;

      String nameToken ="\\p{Upper}(\\p{Lower}+\\s?)";



      String namePattern = "("+nameToken+"){2,3}";

      retval = name.matches(namePattern);

      //prepare a message indicating success or failure
      String msg = "NO MATCH: pattern:" + name
           + "\r\n          regex :" + namePattern;

      if (retval){
      msg = "MATCH     pattern:"  + name
           + "\r\n          regex :" + namePattern;
      }

      System.out.println(msg +"\r\n");
      return retval;
      }
}
```

Output 1-5. Result of Running MatchNameFormats.java

```
C:\RegEx\Examples\chapter1>java MatchNameFormats "John Smith"
MATCH     pattern:John Smith
          regex :(\p{Upper}(\p{Lower}+\s?)){2,3}

C:\RegEx\Examples\chapter1>java MatchNameFormats "John McGee"
MATCH     pattern:John McGee
          regex :(\p{Upper}(\p{Lower}+\s?)){2,3}

C:\RegEx\Examples\chapter1>java MatchNameFormats "John Willliam Smith"
MATCH     pattern:John Willliam Smith
          regex :(\p{Upper}(\p{Lower}+\s?)){2,3}

C:\RegEx\Examples\chapter1>java MatchNameFormats "John Q Smith"
NO MATCH: pattern:John Q Smith
          regex :(\p{Upper}(\p{Lower}+\s?)){2,3}


C:\RegEx\Examples\chapter1>java MatchNameFormats "John allen Smith"
NO MATCH: pattern:John allen Smith
          regex :(\p{Upper}(\p{Lower}+\s?)){2,3}

C:\RegEx\Examples\chapter1>java MatchNameFormats "John"
NO MATCH: pattern:John
          regex :(\p{Upper}(\p{Lower}+\s?)){2,3}
```

Table 1-22. The Pattern (\p{Upper}(\p{Lower}+\s?)){2,3}

Regex	Description
(	A group consisting of
\p{Upper}	An uppercase character
(	Followed by a inner group consisting of
\p{Lower}	A lowercase character
+	Repeated one or more times
\s?	Followed by an optional space
)	The end of the inner group

Table 1-22. The Pattern (\p{Upper}(\p{Lower}+\s?)){2,3} (Continued)

Regex	Description
)	The end of the outer group
{	Repeated at least
2	Two times
,	But no more than
3	Three times
}	End repetition

* **In English:** Look for two or three words beginning with a capital letter followed by any number of lowercase letters. Each word could be followed by a single space.

A couple of questions naturally arise from this example:

- *Why did John Q Public fail?* Because *Q* is not a name token, as you've defined name tokens (i.e., a capital letter followed by one or more lowercase letters).

- *Why did John allen Smith fail?* Because *allen* doesn't start with a capital letter.

- *Why did John fail?* Although *John* is a valid name token, it isn't repeated two or three name tokens. It's simply one name token.

- *Why did John McGee pass? McGee isn't an uppercase letter followed by any number of lowercase letters.* Try to puzzle this one out on your own. It's answered in the "FAQs" section at the end of the chapter.

This example uses the composition technique mentioned at the beginning of this chapter. That is, it uses patterns previous defined to compose a new pattern. If you think about it, this is a very engineer-like thing to do: Build small blocks, then use those blocks to build more complicated pieces.

Confirming Addresses Example

The code in Listing 1-6 simply determines if the given address meets the criterion of being well formatted. It takes advantage of the name and zip code patterns created earlier, and it adds its own address pattern. Output 1-6 shows the result of running the program. Table 1-23 dissects the pattern.

Listing 1-6. MatchAddress.java

```java
import java.util.regex.*;
import java.io.*;

public class MatchAddress{
    public static void main(String args[]){
        isAddressValid(args[0]);
    }

    /**
    * Confirms that the format for the given address is valid.
    * @param addr is a String representing the address
    * @returns true if the zip code format is acceptable.
    */
    public static boolean isAddressValid(String addr){
        boolean retval = false;

        //use the name pattern created earlier.
        String nameToken ="\\p{Upper}(\\p{Lower}+\\s?)";

        String namePattern = "("+nameToken+"){2,3}";

        //use the zip code pattern created earlier.
        String zipCodePattern = "\\d{5}(-\\d{4})?";

        //construct an address pattern
        String addressPattern = "^" + namePattern
            + "\\w+ .*, \\w+ " + zipCodePattern +"$";

        retval= addr.matches(addressPattern);

        //prepare a message indicating success or failure
        String msg = "NO MATCH\npattern:\n " + addr
            + "\nregexLength:\n "
            + addressPattern;

        if (retval){
        msg = "MATCH\npattern:\n " + addr
            + "\nregexLength:\n "
            + addressPattern;
        }
```

```
      System.out.println(msg +"\r\n");
      return retval;
   }
}
```

Output 1-6. Result of Running MatchAddress.java

```
C:\RegEx\chapter_1\Examples\chapter1>
java MatchAddress "John Smith 888 Luck Street,
NY 64332"
MATCH
pattern:
 John Smith 888 Luck Street, NY 64332
regexLength:
 ^(\p{Upper}(\p{Lower}+\s?)){2,3}\w+ .*, \w+ \d{5}(-\d{4})?$


C:\RegEx\chapter_1\Examples\chapter1>
java MatchAddress "John A. Smith 888 Luck Stree
t, NY 64332-4453"
NO MATCH
pattern:
 John A. Smith 888 Luck Street, NY 64332-4453
regexLength:
 ^(\p{Upper}(\p{Lower}+\s?)){2,3}\w+ .*, \w+ \d{5}(-\d{4})?$


C:\RegEx\chapter_1\Examples\chapter1>
java MatchAddress "John Allen Smith 888 Luck Street, NY 64332-4453"
MATCH
pattern:
 John Allen Smith 888 Luck Street, NY 64332-4453
regexLength:
 ^(\p{Upper}(\p{Lower}+\s?)){2,3}\w+ .*, \w+ \d{5}(-\d{4})?$


C:\RegEx\chapter_1\Examples\chapter1>
java MatchAddress "888 Luck Street, NY 64332"
NO MATCH
pattern:
 888 Luck Street, NY 64332
regexLength:
 ^(\p{Upper}(\p{Lower}+\s?)){2,3}\w+ .*, \w+ \d{5}(-\d{4})?$
```

```
C:\RegEx\chapter_1\Examples\chapter1>
java MatchAddress "P.O. BOX 888 Luck Street, NY 64332-4453"
NO MATCH
pattern:
 P.O. BOX 888 Luck Street, NY 64332-4453
regexLength:
 ^(\p{Upper}(\p{Lower}+\s?)){2,3}\w+ .*, \w+ \d{5}(-\d{4})?$


C:\RegEx\chapter_1\Examples\chapter1>
java MatchAddress "John Allen Smith 888 Luck st., NY"
NO MATCH
pattern:
 John Allen Smith 888 Luck st., NY
regexLength:
 ^(\p{Upper}(\p{Lower}+\s?)){2,3}\w+ .*, \w+ \d{5}(-\d{4})?$
```

Table 1-23. The Pattern
^(\p{Upper}(\p{Lower}+\s?)){2,3}\w+ ., \w+ \d{5}(-\d{4})?$*

Regex	Description
^	The beginning of a line followed by
(	A group consisting of
\p{Upper}	An uppercase character
(	Followed by a inner group consisting of
\p{Lower}	A lowercase character
+	Repeated one or more times
\s?	Followed by an optional space
)	The end of the inner group
)	The end of the outer group
{	Repeated at least
2	Two times
,	But no more than
3	Three times

Table 1-23. The Pattern
^(\p{Upper}(\p{Lower}+\s?)){2,3}\w+ .*, \w+ \d{5}(-\d{4})?$ (Continued)

Regex	Description
<space>	Followed by a space
\w	Followed by a any alphanumeric character
+	Repeated one or more times
<space>	Followed by a space
.	Followed by any character
*	Repeated any number of times
,	Followed by a comma
<space>	Followed by a space
\w	Followed by any alphanumeric character
+	Repeated one or more times
<space>	Followed by a space
\d	Followed by a digit
{	Repeated at least
5	Five times
}	End repetition
(	Open group
-	Consisting of a hyphen
\d	A digit
{	Repeated at least
4	Four times
}	End repetition
)	The end of this group
?	Look for zero or one of the preceding

* **In English:** Look for a name token, as previously defined, followed by some words, a comma, and then more words, followed by a zip code. This example uses the composition technique.

Finding Duplicate Words Example

I discussed the code in Listing 1-7 in the "Groups and Back References" section earlier. The point in reintroducing it here is to demonstrate how regular expressions actually interact with Java code.

As you read this example, notice that it uses a `Pattern` and `Matcher`, and not the `String.matches(regex)` method, as most of the examples in the previous sections have. Try to guess why this approach has been taken. For the answer, look in the "FAQs" section at the end of this chapter. Output 1-7 shows the result of running the program. The pattern is dissected in Table 1-24.

Listing 1-7. MatchDuplicateWords.java

```java
import java.util.regex.*;
import java.io.*;

public class MatchDuplicateWords{
    public static void main(String args[]){
        hasDuplicate(args[0]);
    }

    /**
    * Confirms that given phrase avoids duplicate words.
    * @param phrase is a String representing the phrase.
    * @returns true if the phrase avoids duplicate
    * words.
    */
    public static boolean hasDuplicate(String phrase){
        boolean retval=false;

        String duplicatePattern =
        "\\b(\\w+) \\1\\b";
```

```java
    // Compile the pattern
    Pattern p = null;
    try{
      p = Pattern.compile(duplicatePattern);
    }
    catch (PatternSyntaxException pex){
        pex.printStackTrace();
        System.exit(0);
    }
    //count the number of matches.
    int matches = 0;

    //get the matcher
    Matcher m = p.matcher(phrase);
    String val=null;

    //find all matching Strings
    while (m.find()){
       retval = true;
      val =  ":" + m.group() +":";
      System.out.println(val);
      matches++;
    }

    //prepare a message indicating success or failure
    String msg = "   NO MATCH: pattern:" + phrase
          + "\r\n            regex: "
          + duplicatePattern;

    if (retval){
    msg = "   MATCH   : pattern:" + phrase
        + "\r\n            regex: "
        + duplicatePattern;
    }

    System.out.println(msg +"\r\n");
    return retval;
  }
}
```

Output 1-7. Result of Running MatchDuplicateWords.java

```
C:\RegEx\Examples\chapter1>java MatchDuplicateWords "pizza pizza"
:pizza pizza:
   MATCH    : pattern:pizza pizza
             regex: \b(\w+) \1\b

C:\RegEx\Examples\chapter1>java MatchDuplicateWords "Faster pussycat kill kill"
:kill kill:
   MATCH    : pattern:Faster pussycat kill kill
             regex: \b(\w+) \1\b

C:\RegEx\Examples\chapter1>java MatchDuplicateWords "The mayor of of simpleton"
:of of:
   MATCH    : pattern:The mayor of of simpleton
             regex: \b(\w+) \1\b

C:\RegEx\Examples\chapter1>java MatchDuplicateWords "Never Never Never Never Never"
:Never Never:
:Never Never:
   MATCH    : pattern:Never Never Never Never Never
             regex: \b(\w+) \1\b

C:\RegEx\Examples\chapter1>java MatchDuplicateWords "222 2222"
   NO MATCH: pattern:222 2222
             regex: \b(\w+) \1\b

C:\RegEx\Examples\chapter1>java MatchDuplicateWords "sara sarah"
   NO MATCH: pattern:sara sarah
             regex: \b(\w+) \1\b

C:\RegEx\Examples\chapter1>java MatchDuplicateWords "Faster pussycat kill, kill"
   NO MATCH: pattern:Faster pussycat kill, kill
             regex: \b(\w+) \1\b

C:\RegEx\Examples\chapter1>java MatchDuplicateWords ". ."
   NO MATCH: pattern:. .
             regex: \b(\w+) \1\b
```

Table 1-24. The Pattern \b(\w+) \1\b

Regex	Description
\b	A word boundary
(	Followed by a group consisting of
\w	An alphanumeric or underscore character
+	Repeated one or more times
)	Close group
<space>	Followed by a space
\1	Followed by the exact group of characters captured previously
\b	Followed by a word boundary

* **In English:** Look for a word boundary, followed by a group of alphanumeric characters, followed by a space, followed by the *exact same group of alphanumeric characters found previously,* followed by a word boundary. In short, look for duplicate words.

Regular Expression Operations

In this section, you'll explore slightly more realistic uses of regular expressions. In the practical world, people use regular expressions for one of three basic broad categories:

- *Data validation:* This is the process of making sure that your candidate String conforms to a specific format (e.g., making sure passwords are at least eight characters long and contain at least two digits).

- *Search and/or replace:* This is another popular usage of regular expressions, and for good reason. Say you want to send a letter to all of your customers, and you want each letter to be personalized by interspersing the customer's name throughout the letter. Of course, this is a little more complex than it sounds, because different names have different lengths, and you don't want to overwrite the next word in your letter when you insert a longer name. Regex is a perfect solution for these types of problems.

- *Decomposing text:* This can also be a challenging activity, particularly if the String in question needs to be split according to complex rules. Fortunately, doing so becomes much easier with regular expressions, as Listing 1-11 (which follows shortly) demonstrates.

Data Validation

Data validation, or making sure that data matches a prescribed format, is one of the most common uses for regular expressions. This can be particularly challenging because data often takes inexact forms and is defined by unspoken rules.

J2SE 1.4 offers you several ways to validate data. The easiest is using the new method `boolean String.matches(String regex)`. This method confirms that the pattern passed in *exactly* matches the `String` that it's called on.

This exactness can be tricky, so it's important to understand it well. For example, say you need to confirm that a given `String` contains the word *Java*, followed by space, followed by some digit. Further, assume that your candidate `String` is `I love Java 4`. The next section demonstrates the process of working through this example.

Data Validation with Strings Example

This example seems simple enough, so you start out by testing the pattern *Java \d*. Table 1-25 shows a breakdown of the pattern.

*Table 1-25. The Pattern **Java \d***

Regex	Description
J	A capital *J*
a	Followed the character *a*
v	Followed the character *v*
a	Followed the character *a*
<space>	Followed by a single space
\d	Followed by digit

That was pretty easy, so you confidently write your code, as shown in Listing 1-8.

Listing 1-8. ValidationTest.java

```
import java.util.regex.*;

public class ValidationTest{
    public static void main(String args[]){
        String candidate = "I love Java 4";
        String pattern ="Java \\d";
        System.out.println(candidate.matches(pattern));
    }
}
```

Then you run it:

```
java ValidationTest
```

and you watch it fail in Output 1-8.

Output 1-8. Result of Running ValidationTest.java

```
C:\RegEx\code>java ValidationTest
Does candidate : I love Java 4
match pattern  : Java \d?

false
```

What happened? Because your input string is I love Java 4, and the Java 4 is preceded by I love, the input isn't an exact match to the pattern *Java \d*. It's a partial match. So what do you do now?

You have two options. You could modify the pattern to allow for characters before and/or after the Java 4 you want to match on, or you could just use the Pattern and Matcher objects. Let's explore the pros and cons of each option.

To use the String.matcher(String regex) method, you need to account for any and all characters that might precede or follow the pattern *Java \d*. Thus, you use the pattern *.*\bJava \d(|$)*, which Table 1-26 dissects.

Table 1-26. The Pattern .*\bJava \d(|$)

Regex	Description
.	Any character
*	Repeated any number of times
\b	Followed by a word boundary
J	Followed by a capital *J*
a	Followed the character *a*
v	Followed the character *v*
a	Followed the character *a*
<space>	Followed by a single space
\d	Followed by a digit
(	Followed by a group consisting of
<space>	A space
|	Or
$	An end-of-line character
)	Close group

Data Validation with the Pattern and Matcher Objects Example

Writing the pattern in the preceding section involved a little bit more work than expected. Let's see if it's any easier to use the Pattern and Marcher objects in Listing 1-9. The output is shown in Output 1-9.

Listing 1-9. ValidationTestWithPatternAndMatcher.java

```
import java.util.regex.*;

public class ValidationTestWithPatternAndMatcher{
    public static void main(String args[]){
```

```
    // Compile the pattern
    Pattern p = null;
    try{
      p = Pattern.compile("Java \\d");
    }
    catch (PatternSyntaxException pex){
        pex.printStackTrace();
        System.exit(0);
    }

    //define the matcher string

    String candidate = "I love Java 4";
    //get the matcher
    Matcher m = p.matcher(candidate);

    System.out.println("result=" + m.find());
    }
}
```

Output 1-9. Result of Running ValidationTestWithPatternAndMatcher.java

```
C:\RegEx\Examples\chapter1>java
ValidationTestWithPatternAndMatcher
result = true
```

The pattern used in Listing 1-9 is less complicated than that in Listing 1-8. It's simply the original string *Java \d*. But the Java code requires explicit usage of the Pattern and Matcher objects, which is slightly more demanding of the programmer. You're doing this because you want explicit access to the Matcher.find method, which allows you to examine the input string and see if any part of it matches the pattern. Again, this in contrast to the String.matches(String regex) method, which requires an exact match.

Generally speaking, there are two types of validation. The first type requires an exact match. For these, the easiest validation method is probably to use the String.matches(String regex), because it rejects anything that doesn't match fully and completely.

The second type of validation requires that the string contain the pattern at some point, but it doesn't require an exact match. For example, you might require that a password contain nonalphanumeric characters. These types of validations are best achieved by using the `Matcher` and `Pattern` objects. Chapter 5 provides more complex validation examples.

Search and Replace

One of the most powerful features of the new regex package is the ability to search for and replace Strings and substrings. As you may recall, this sort of activity was previously a tedious affair, as it required the use of tokenizers or the use of the `String.substring` methods, along with a lot of `String` arithmetic.

Thankfully, those days are over. There are two general ways to do search and replace operations in J2SE. The following example travels the easier path by taking advantage of two new methods added to the `String` class. (Chapter 4 contains more complex examples that use the `Pattern` and `Matcher` classes directly.) The two methods relevant for the following example are as follows:

- `replaceFirst(String regex, String replacement)`

- `replaceAll(String regex,String replacement)`

The first method, `replaceFirst(String regex, String replacement)`, simply replaces the first occurrence of the regex pattern with the replacement `String`. The second method, `replaceAll`, replaces *all* occurrences of the pattern with the replacement `String`. I explain these new methods in detail in Chapter 2.

Search and Replace Example

If you're like me, you probably think about programming more than you should. Say you're writing an essay on boxing. Further, say you decide to update your essay on boxing programmatically instead of manually. Listing 1-10 shows the code for doing so. The example searches for and replaces some commonly misused phrases from the given paragraph. Output 1-10 shows the result of running the program.

Listing 1-10. StyleSearchAndReplace.java

```
public class StyleSearchAndReplace{
  public static void main(String args[]){

    String statement = "The question as to whether the jab is"+
    " superior to the cross has been debated for some time in"+
    " boxing circles. However, it is my opinion that this"+
```

```
" false dichotomy misses the point. I call your attention"+
" to the fact that the best boxers often use a combination of"+
" the two. I call your attention to the fact that Mohammed"+
" Ali,the Greatest of the sport of boxing, used both. He had"+
" a tremendous jab, yet used his cross effectively, often,"+
" and well";

String newStmt=
statement.replaceAll("The question as to whether","Whether");

newStmt= newStmt.replaceAll(" of the sport of boxing","");
newStmt=newStmt.replaceAll("amount of success","success");
newStmt=
 newStmt.replaceAll("However, it is my opinion that this","This");

newStmt= newStmt.replaceAll("a combination of the two","both");
newStmt= newStmt.replaceAll("This is in spite of the fact that"
 +" the", "The");
newStmt=
 newStmt.replaceAll("I call your attention to the fact that","");

System.out.println("BEFORE:\n"+statement + "\n");
System.out.println("AFTER:\n"+newStmt);
 }
}
```

Output 1-10. Result of Running StyleSearchAndReplace.java

```
C:\RegEx\Examples\chapter1>java StyleSearchAndReplace
BEFORE:
The question as to whether the jab is superior to the cross has been debated for
some time in boxing circles. However, it is my opinion that this false dichotomy
misses the point. I call your attention to the fact that the best boxers often
use a combination of the two. I call your attention to the fact that Mohammed
Ali,the Greatest of the sport of boxing, used both. He had a tremendous jab, yet
used his cross effectively,often, and well
AFTER:

Whether the jab is superior to the cross has been debated for some time in boxing
circles. This false dichotomy misses the point.  the best boxers often use both.
Mohammed Ali,the Greatest, used both. He had a tremendous jab, yet used his cross
effectively,often, and well
```

As Output 1-10 shows, the clarity of the paragraph has improved somewhat as a result of this process.

Splitting a String

There are many mechanisms available for splitting a String, the most obvious being the StringTokenizer. However, splitting a String can be surprisingly complex, because it can require fairly complex criteria. For example, it's easy enough to split a comma-separated file, but what about splitting a word into vowels and consonants? The latter can be ridiculously complicated. Fortunately, regular expressions can be particularly helpful in these sorts of situations, as you'll learn in the following sections.

Splitting a String Example

In English rhetoric, we learn that one of the best ways to strengthen a sentence is to place positives and negatives in opposition. The code in Listing 1-11 takes a sentence and attempts to strengthen it by placing the positives and negatives in opposition. Output 1-11 shows the result.

Listing 1-11. StyleSplitExample.java

```java
public class StyleSplitExample{
   public static void main(String args[]){
      String phrase1= "but simple justice, not charity";
      strengthenSentence(phrase1);

      String phrase2=
        "but that I love Rome more, not that I love Caesar less";
      strengthenSentence(phrase2);

      String phrase3=
      "ask what you can do for your country, ask not what your "
      + "country can do for you";
      strengthenSentence(phrase3);
   }
```

```
/**
 * Splits and rearranges the given String, hopefully to a more
 * powerful effect.
 * @param sentence is a String representing the phrase we want to
 * strengthen.
 * @returns is a String representing the modified phrase.
 */
public static String strengthenSentence(String sentence){
    String retval=null;

    String[] tokens = null;

    String splitPattern =  ",";

    tokens= sentence.split(splitPattern);

    if (tokens==null){
        String msg = "   NO MATCH: pattern:" + sentence
            + "\r\n               regex: " + splitPattern;
    }
    else{
        retval = tokens[1] + ", " + tokens[0];
        System.out.println("BEFORE: " + sentence);
        System.out.println("AFTER : " + retval +"\n");
    }
    return retval;
  }
}
```

Output 1-11. Result of Running StyleSplitExample.java

```
C:\RegEx\Examples\chapter1>java StyleSplitExample
BEFORE: but simple justice, not charity
AFTER :  not charity, but simple justice

BEFORE: but that I love Rome more, not that I love Caesar less
AFTER :  not that I love Caesar less, but that I love Rome more

BEFORE: ask what you can do for your country, ask not what your
country can do for you
AFTER :  ask not what your country can do for you, ask what you can
do for your country
```

Conditional String Splitting Example

Regex becomes particularly useful when you have more complete String parsing needs. It's easy enough to split a string when it's in a well-defined format, such as a comma-delimited file. You don't need regex for that; a StringTokenizer will do just fine. But what if you want to split a string based on, say, a word or any of its synonyms?

Regular expressions can be helpful in these kinds of scenarios because they allow you to qualify complex criteria for effecting a division. Listing 1-12 splits the given phrase based on occurrences of the word *compromise* or its synonyms. Output 1-12 shows the result of running the program.

Listing 1-12. Split.java

```java
public class Split{
    public static void main(String args[]){

        String statement = "I will not compromise. I will not "+
        "cooperate. There will be no concession, no conciliation, no "+
        "finding the middle group, and no give and take.";

        String tokens[]  =null;

        String splitPattern= "compromise|coopcratc|concession|"+
        "conciliation|(finding the middle group)|(give and take)";

        tokens=statement.split(splitPattern);

        System.out.println("REGEX PATTERN:\n"+splitPattern + "\n");

        System.out.println("STATEMENT:\n"+statement + "\n");
        System.out.println("\nTOKENS");
        for (int i=0; i < tokens.length; i++){
        System.out.println(tokens[i]);
        }
    }
}
```

Output 1-12. Result of Running Split.java

```
C:\RegEx\Examples\chapter1>java Split
REGEX PATTERN:
compromise|cooperate|concession|conciliation|(finding the middle group)|(give
and take)

STATEMENT:
I will not compromise. I will not cooperate. There will be no
concession, no conciliation,
 no finding the middle group, and no give and take.

TOKENS:
I will not
. I will not
. There will be no
, no
, no
, and no
.
```

This example illustrates the new types of possibilities that now exist as part of the standard Java implementation. I discuss more sophisticated splits in Chapters 3 and 4.

Comparing Regex and Perl

Perl is probably the most popular language to offer regular expression support. As such, it makes sense to put Java's regex support in context by comparing it to that of Perl. The distinctions you should be aware of are highlighted in the sections that follow. Generally speaking, J2SE doesn't include some Perl constructs, because Java is a full-featured programming language that offers sophisticated condition and logical paths of execution that are reasonable alternatives to the constructs offered by Perl.

What Perl Offers That Java Regex Doesn't

There are several constructs and concepts you might be familiar with from your Perl experience that you won't be able to use in the current implementation of Java. Because these are parts of Perl and not Java, I mention them only briefly here.

Regex String modification isn't supported in Java. This means that you can't modify a String with regex. Strings are immutable objects in Java, so you'll have to use methods that return a new String with the modifications you need. In addition, you'll have to modify your String manually, as opposed to using regex patterns to do so. The earlier search and replace example shows how this works. The original String isn't modified—it simply returns a new String that represents the modification.

Perl's conditional constructs, *(?{X})* and *(?(condition)X|Y)*, aren't supported by J2SE's regex. Because Java offers robust if-then-else support as a language feature, there's no need for conditional constructs. Chapter 4 provides examples of how this works.

Java doesn't support the embedded code constructs *(?(code))* and *(??(code))*. Again, these are the sorts of things that can be handled more intuitively, by Java standards, by using Java's built-in language features.

Java doesn't support embedded comments by default, because your patterns can be so easily commented when you create them as Strings. However, you can use the Pattern.COMMENT flag to compile your regex with comments if you really need to. For more on this, please see Chapter 2.

Java doesn't support the preprocessing operations *\l \u, \L,* and *\U.*

What Java Regex Offers That Perl Doesn't

Possessive qualifiers are unique to Java, but they're very likely to be adopted by other regex implementations soon, because they're such a good idea. Possessive qualifiers continue to retain any qualifying greedy match. That means that once a possessive match is achieved, it isn't relinquished. I discuss possessive qualifiers in depth in Chapter 3.

Summary

This chapter covered some general regex syntax and introduced the concepts of the Matcher and Pattern classes. You learned some methods for creating your own regular expressions and how you might actually use them in Java. Finally, you explored some concrete examples and reasoned your way through them. Chapter 2 continues to build on this theme and provide you with a deeper understanding of Java's regex package.

Q: The \b metacharacter seems to act inconsistently in regular expressions as I write them. What's going on?

A: In regex, \b means a word boundary. However, in general Java vernacular, \b means a backspace. Here's the rule: The literal String \b means a backspace character. However, the literal String \\b means a word boundary.

Q: When should I use the String.matches method instead of the Pattern and Matcher objects directly?

A: Use the String.matches method if you require an exact match. For example, if you want exactly seven consecutive digits and nothing else is acceptable, then use String.matches with the pattern \d{7}. In general, if you're prepared to narrow the definition of acceptable patterns, or if you're willing to define every possible variation, then use the String.matches method. On the other hand, if you're looking for the existence of substring, you're better served by the Pattern and Matcher objects.

Q: Is using the String.matches method less resource-intensive than using the Pattern and Matcher objects?

A: No. The String.matches method simply calls the Pattern.matches method, which in turn creates and uses both a Pattern object and a Matcher object.

Q: Can I modify a String by applying a regular expression to it?

A: Absolutely not. Strings are immutable objects in Java, and thus they cannot be changed. However, you can create a new String object that has the requested changes. Thus, if you have

```
String tmp = "Hello";
```

and you want to change the e to a X by doing the following:

```
String newTmp = tmp.replaceFirst("e","X");
```

the value of tmp is still Hello, but the value of newTmp is HXllo.

Q: Why did the pattern (\p{Upper}(\p{Lower}+\s?)){2,3} match John McGee in the NameFormat.java example?

A: Because *John* meets the first part of the pattern, *Mc* meets the second part of the pattern, and *Gee* meets the second part of the pattern. As a test, try running *John Janis McGee* through the NameFormat.java program.

The point here is that *John* consists of an uppercase letter, followed by one or more lowercase letters, followed by one space. *Mc* consists of an uppercase letter, followed by one or more lowercase letters, followed by no space, and *Gee* consists of an uppercase letter, followed by one or more lowercase letters, followed by no space. This isn't exactly what you may have had in mind, but it seems permissible in this case. It's very important to be precise and do a lot of testing when working with regular expressions, or unexpected results are sure to follow.

Q: What type of regex engine does Java use?

A: J2SE uses a traditional nondeterministic finite automaton (NFA) engine. This means that when the engine reaches a fork in the road, it chooses one path, remembers where the other path is in case things don't work out, and goes from there.

The advantage here is that you could be leading the engine to a match very, very quickly if you write efficient expressions. The disadvantage is that you could be leading the regex engine on a wild goose chase before it finally gets the match by writing inefficient expressions.

CHAPTER 2

Introduction to the Java.util.regex Object Model

"How do you eat an elephant? One bite at a time."
— Proverb

JAVA'S NEW java.util.regex package offers an elegant and agile object model with which to meet regular expression needs. It is composed, in its entirety, of three objects: the Pattern object, the Matcher object, and a PatternSyntaxException. This chapter details all of the methods and fields of the Pattern and Matcher classes, and provides examples of their use. In this chapter I also discuss the new regular expression supportive methods retrofitted into the String class.

The chapter starts with an examination of the Pattern class. I cover every method and field and often provide examples. I also explore the Matcher class in similar detail. Finally, I round out the chapter by discussing the regex methods that have been added to the String class.

The Pattern Object

Figure 2-1 shows the methods of the Pattern class. The figure is a UML rendering of the Pattern class that illustrates the various methods and constants of the class.

```
┌─────────────────────────────────────────────────────────────┐
│                           Pattern                            │
├─────────────────────────────────────────────────────────────┤
│ +CANON_EQ:int=128                                            │
│ +CASE_INSENSITIVE:int=2                                       │
│ +COMMENTS:INT=4                                               │
│ +DOTALL:INT=32                                                │
│ +MULTILINE:int=8                                              │
│ +UNICODE_CASE:INT=64                                          │
│ +UNIX_LINE:INT=1                                              │
├─────────────────────────────────────────────────────────────┤
│ +compile(regex:String):Pattern                               │
│ +compile(regex:String,flags:int):Pattern                     │
│ +flags():int                                                 │
│ +matcher(input:CharSequence):Matcher                         │
│ +matches(regex:String,input:CharSequence):boolean            │
│ +pattern():String                                            │
│ +split(input:CharSequence):String[]                          │
│ +split(input:CharSequence,limit:int):String[]                │
└─────────────────────────────────────────────────────────────┘
```

Figure 2-1. A UML representation of the Pattern class

Let's examine the fields and methods of the Pattern class in detail. If you aren't familiar with UML, here's a quick guide to reading Figure 2-1:

- The name of the class is Pattern, and it's in the topmost section of the rectangle.

- The middle section is a grouping of the field variables. The plus sign (+) preceding these indicates that they're public. The underline indicates that they're static, and the ": int" indicates that they're of type int. The "= num" indicates the default value.

- The bottommost section of the rectangle holds the class's methods. Again, the plus sign indicates public access, and the underline indicates that the method is static. The parentheses designate the parameters for a given method; thus, flags() takes no parameters, whereas matcher(input : CharSequence) takes variable named input of type CharSequence. The colon (:) toward the end indicates a type.

The following sections describe the fields and methods of the Pattern class.

public static final int UNIX_LINES

The `UNIX_LINES` flag is used in constructing the second parameter of the
`Pattern.compile(String regex, int flags)` method. Use this flag when you parse
data that originates on a UNIX machine.

On many flavors of UNIX, the invisible character *n* is used to note termination
of a line. This is distinct from other operating systems, including flavors of Windows,
which may use *r**n*, *n*, *r*, *u2028*, or *u0085* for a line terminator.

If you transport a file that originated on a UNIX machine to a Windows platform
and open it, you may notice that the lines will sometimes not terminate in the
expected manner, depending on which editor you use to view the text. This happens
because the two systems can use different syntax to denote the end of a line.

The `UNIX_LINES` flag simply tells the regex engine that it's dealing with UNIX-style
lines, which affects the matching behavior of the regular expression metacharacters
∧ and *$*. Using the `UNIX_LINES` flag, or the equivalent *(?d)* regex pattern, doesn't
degrade performance. By default, this flag isn't set.

public static final int CASE_INSENSITIVE

The `CASE_INSENSITIVE` field is used when constructing the second parameter of the
`Pattern.compile(String regex, int flags)` method. It's useful when you need to
match ASCII characters, regardless of case.

Using this flag or the equivalent *(?I)* regular expression can cause performance
to degrade slightly. By default, this flag isn't set.

public static final int COMMENTS

The `COMMENTS` flag is used in constructing the second parameter of the
`Pattern.compile(String regex, int flags)` method. It tells the regex engine that
the regex pattern has an embedded comment in it. Specifically, it tells the regex
engine to ignore any comments in the pattern, starting with the spaces leading up
to the # character and everything thereafter, until the end of the line.

Thus, the regex pattern *A   #matches uppercase US-ASCII char code 65* will
use *A* as the regular expression, but the spaces leading to the # character and
everything after it until the end of the line will be ignored. Your code might end up
looking something like this:

```
Pattern p =
Pattern.compile("A    #matches uppercase US-ASCII char code 65",Pattern.COMMENTS);
```

Think of the # character as the regex equivalent of the java comment //. By using the COMMENTS flag in compiling your regex, you're telling the regex engine that your expression contains comments, which should be ignored. This can be useful if your pattern is particularly complex or subtle. When you don't set this flag, the regex engine will attempt to interpret and use your comments as part of the regular expression.

Using this flag or the equivalent *(?x)* regular expression doesn't degrade performance.

public static final int MULTILINE

The MULTILINE flag is used in constructing the second parameter of the Pattern.compile(String regex, int flags) method. It tells the regex engine that regex input isn't a single line of code; rather, it contains several lines that have their own termination characters.

This means that the beginning-of-line character, ^, and the end-of-line character, $, will potentially match several lines within the input String. For example, imagine that your input String is *This is a sentence.\n So is this.*. If you use the MULTILINE flag to compile the regular expression pattern

```
Pattern p = Pattern.compile("^", Pattern.MULTILINE);
```

then the beginning of line character, ^, will match before the *T* in *This is a sentence.* It will also match just before the *S* in *So is this.* When you don't use the MULTILINE flag, the match will only find the *T* in *This is a sentence.*

Using this flag or the equivalent *(?m)* regular expression may degrade performance.

public static final int DOTALL

The DOTALL flag is used in constructing the second parameter of the Pattern.compile(String regex, int flags) method. The DOTALL flag tells the regex engine to allow the metacharacter period to match any character, including line termination characters. What does this mean?

Imagine that your candidate String is *Test\n*. If your corresponding regex pattern is **.** you would normally have four matches: one for the *T*, another for the *e*, another for *s*, and the fourth for *t*. This is because the regex metacharacter **.** will normally match any character *except* a line termination character.

Enabling the DOTALL flag as follows:

```
Pattern p = Pattern.compile(".", Pattern.DOTALL);
```

would generate five matches. Your pattern would match the *T, e, s,* and *t* characters. In addition, it would match the *\n* character at the end of the line.

Using this flag or the equivalent *(?s)* regular expression doesn't degrade performance.

public static final int UNICODE_CASE

The UNICODE_CASE flag is used in constructing the second parameter of the Pattern.compile(String regex, int flags) method. It is used in conjunction with the CASE_INSENITIVE flag to generate case-insensitive matches for the international character sets.

Using this flag or the equivalent *(?u)* regular expression can degrade performance.

public static final int CANON_EQ

The CANON_EQ flag is used in constructing the second parameter of the Pattern.compile(String regex, int flags) method. As you know, characters are actually stored as numbers. For example, in the ASCII character set, the character *A* is represented by the number 65. Depending on the character set that you're using, the same character can be represented by different numeric combinations. For example, *à* can be represented by both *+00E0* and *U+0061U+0300*. A CANON_EQ match would match either representation.

Using this flag may degrade performance.

public static Pattern compile(String regex) Throws a PatternSyntaxException

You'll notice that the Pattern class doesn't have a public constructor. This means that you *can't* write the following type of code:

```
Pattern p = new Pattern("my regex");//wrong!
```

To get a reference to a Pattern object, you must use the static method compile(String regex). Thus, your first line of regex code might look like the following:

```
Pattern p = Pattern.compile("my regex");//Right!
```

The parameter for this method is a String that represents a regular expression. When you pass a String to a method that expects a regular expression, it's important to delimit any \ characters that the regular expressions might have by appending another \ character to them. This is because String objects internally use the \ character to delimit metacharacters in character sequences, regardless of whether those character sequences are regular expressions. This was true long before regular expressions were part of Java. Thus, the regular expression \d becomes \\d. To match a single digit, your regular expression becomes the following:

```
Pattern p = Pattern.compile("\\d");
```

The point here being that the regular expression *\d* becomes the String \\d.

The delimitation of the String parameter can sometimes be tricky, so it's important to understand it well. By and large, it means that you *double* the \ characters that might already be present in the regular expression. It *does not mean* that you simply append a single \ character. I present an example to illustrate this shortly.

The compile method will throw a java.util.regex.PatternSyntaxException if the regular expression itself is badly formed. For example, if you pass in a String that contains *[4*, the compile method will throw a PatternSyntaxException at runtime, because the syntax of the regular expression *[4* is illegal, as shown in Listing 2-1.

Listing 2-1. Using the compile Method

```
import java.util.regex.*;

public class DelimitTest{
  public static void main(String args[]){


    //throws exception
    Pattern p = Pattern.compile("[4");
  }
}
```

Does this mean that you have to catch a PatternSyntaxException every time you use a regular expression? No. PatternSyntaxException doesn't have to be explicitly caught, because it extends from a RuntimeException, and a RuntimeException doesn't need to be explicitly caught.

The compile(String regex) method returns a Pattern object.

public static Pattern compile(String regex, int flags) Throws a PatternSyntaxException

The (String regex, int flags) method is a more powerful form of the compile(String) method. The first parameter for this method, regex, is a String that represents a regular expression, as detailed in the Pattern.compile(String regex) method presented earlier. For details on how you must format the String parameter, please see the "public static Pattern compile(String regex) Throws a PatternSyntaxException" section.

The flexibility of this compile method is fully realized by using the second parameter, int flags. The int flags parameter can consist of the following flags or a bit mask created by OR-ing combinations thereof:

- CANON_EQ

- CASE_INSENSTIVE

- COMMENTS

- DOTALL

- MULTILINE

- UNICODE_CASE

- UNIX_LINES

For example, if you want a match to be successful regardless of the case of the candidate String, then your pattern might look like the following:

```
Pattern p = Pattern.compile(regex,Pattern.CASE_INSENSITIVE);
```

You can combine the flags by using the | operator. For example, to achieve case-insensitive Unicode matches that include a comment, you might use the following:

```
Pattern p =
Pattern.compile("t # a compound flag example",
Pattern.CASE_INSENSITIVE | Pattern.UNICODE_CASE|
Pattern.COMMENT);
```

The compile(String regex, int flags) method returns a Pattern object.

public String pattern()

This method returns a simple String representation of the regex compiled. It can sometimes be misleading in two ways. First, the string that's returned doesn't reflect any flags that were set when the pattern was compiled. Second, the regex String you pass in isn't always the pattern String you get back out. Specifically, the original String delimitations aren't shown. Thus, if your original code was this:

```
Pattern p = Pattern.compile("\\d");
```

you should expect your output to be *\d*, with a single \ character.

A question naturally arises here: If this method strips out the original delimiting, can you use the resulting String as a regular expression to feed another expression? For example, does Listing 2-2 work?

Listing 2-2. Pattern Matching Example

```
import java.util.regex.*;

public class PatternMethodExample{
  public static void main(String args[]){
      reusePatternMethodExample();
  }

    public static void reusePatternMethodExample(){
       //match a single digit
       Pattern p = Pattern.compile("\\d");
       Matcher matcher = p.matcher("5");
       boolean isOk = matcher.matches();
       System.out.println("original pattern matches " + isOk);

       //recycle the pattern
       String tmp = p.pattern();
       Pattern p2 = Pattern.compile(tmp);
       matcher = p.matcher("5");
       isOk = matcher.matches();
       System.out.println("second pattern matches " + isOk);
    }
}
```

Will this method throw a RuntimeException? After all, the pattern() method returns *\d*, and an attempt to create a regex pattern using *\d* as a String will fail to compile.

The answer is no, it won't throw an exception. Remember that the doubling of the \ character is a requirement of the String object's constructor—it has nothing to do with the regex pattern that the String represents. Thus, once the String is created, the conflict disintegrates.

public Matcher matcher(CharSequence input)

Remember that you create a Pattern object by compiling a description of what you're looking for. A Pattern is a bit like a personal ad: It lists the features of the thing you're looking for. Speaking purely conceptually, your patterns might look like the following:

```
Pattern p = Pattern.compile("She must have red hair, and a temper");
```

Correspondingly, you'll need to compare that description against candidates. That is, you'll want to examine a given String to see if it matches the description you provided.

The Matcher object is designed specifically to help you do this sort of interrogation. I discuss Matcher in detail in the next major section of this chapter, but for now you should know that the Pattern.matcher(CharSequence input) method returns the Matcher that will help get details about how your candidate String compares with the description you passed in.

Pattern.matcher(CharSequence input) takes a CharSequence parameter as an input parameter. CharSequence is a new interface introduced in J2SE 1.4 and retroactively implemented by the String object. Because String implements CharSequence, you can simply pass a String object as the parameter to the Pattern.matcher(CharSequence input) method. I discuss the CharSequence parameter in detail shortly.

In the preceding example, again speaking purely conceptually, you might get your Matcher object as follows:

```
Matcher m = pattern.matches("Anna");
```

In J2SE, this Matcher object's matches() would return true. In real life, YMMV.

public int flags()

Earlier I discussed the constant flags that you can use in compiling your regex pattern. The flags method simply returns an int that represents those flags. For example, to see whether your Pattern class is currently using a given flag (say, the Pattern.COMMENTS flag), simply extract the flag:

```
int flgs  = myPattern.flags();
```

then "and" (&) that flag to the `Pattern.COMMENTS` flag:

```
boolean isUsingCommentFlag =(  Pattern.COMMENTS == (Pattern.COMMENTS & flgs)) ;
```

Similarly, to see if you're using the `CASE_INSENSITIVE` flag, use the following code:

```
boolean isUsingCaseInsensitiveFlag =
(Pattern.CASE_INSENSITIVE == (Pattern. CASE_INSENSITIVE & flgs));
```

public static boolean matches (String regex,CharSequence input)

Very often, you'll find that all you need to know about a `String` is whether it matches a given regular expression exactly. You don't want to have to create a `Pattern` object, extract its `Matcher` object, and interrogate that `Matcher`.

This static utility method is designed to do exactly that. Internally, it creates the `Pattern` and `Matcher` objects you need, compares the regex to the input `String`, and returns a boolean that tells you whether the two match exactly. Listing 2-3 presents an example of its use.

Listing 2-3. Matches Example

```
import java.util.regex.*;
public class PatternMatchesTest{
  public static void main(String args[]){

      String regex = "ad*";
      String input = "add";

      boolean isMatch = Pattern.matches(regex,input);
      System.out.println(isMatch);//return true
  }
}
```

If you're going to do a lot of comparisons, then it's more efficient to explicitly create a `Pattern` object and do your matches manually. However, if you aren't going to do a lot of comparisons, then `matches` is a handy utility method.

The `Pattern.matches(String regex, CharSequence input)` method is also used internally by the `String` class. As of J2SE 1.4, `String` has a new method called `matches` that internally defers to the `Pattern.matches` method. You might already be using this method without being aware of it.

Of course, this method can throw a `PatternSyntaxException` if the regex pattern under consideration isn't well formed.

public String[] split(CharSequence input)

This method can be particularly helpful if you need to break up a `String` into an array of substrings based on some criteria. In concept, it's similar to the `StringTokenizer`, but it's much more powerful and more resource intensive than `StringTokenizer` because it allows your program to use regular expressions as the splitting criteria.

This method always returns at least one element. If the split candidate, `input`, can't be found, then a `String` array is returned that contains exactly one `String`—namely, the original `input`.

If the `input` can be found, then a `String` array is returned. That array contains every substring after an occurrence of the `input`. Thus, for the pattern

```
Pattern p = new Pattern.compile(",");
```

the split method for *Hello, Dolly* will return a `String` array consisting of two elements. The first element of the array will contain *Hello*, and the second will contain *Dolly*. That `String` array is obtained as follows:

```
String tmp[] = p.split("Hello,Dolly");
```

In this case, the value returned is

```
//tmp is equal to { "Hello", "Dolly"}
```

You should be aware of some subtleties when you work with this method. If the candidate `String` had been *Hello,Dolly,* with a trailing comma character after the *y* in *Dolly* then this method would still have returned a two-element `String` array consisting of *Hello* and *Dolly*. The implicit behavior is that trailing spaces aren't returned.

If the input `String` had been *Hello,,,Dolly* the resulting `String` array would have had four elements. The return value of the split method, as applied to the pattern, is

```
// p.split("Hello,,,Dolly") returns {"Hello","","","Dolly"}
```

Listing 2-4 provides an example in which the split method is used to split a String into an array based on a single space character.

Listing 2-4. Pattern Splitting Example

```
import java.util.regex.*;
public class PatternSplitExample{
  public static void main(String args[]){
      splitTest();
  }

  public static void splitTest(){

    Pattern p =
    Pattern.compile(" ");
    String tmp = "this is the String I want to split up";

    String[] tokens = p.split(tmp);

    for (int i=0; i<tokens.length; i++ ){
      System.out.println(tokens[i]);
    }

  }
}
```

Of course, this is a misuse of the method: You could have used a StringTokenizer to achieve the same result, and it would have been less resource intensive. In light of what you now know, consider Listing 2-5, which is a slightly modified version of Listing 1-12 from Chapter 1 in that it uses the Pattern.split method. Output 2-1 shows the result of running the program.

Listing 2-5. PatternSplit.java

```
import java.util.regex.*;

public class PatternSplit{
    public static void main(String args[]){

        String statement = "I will not compromise. I will not "+
        "cooperate. There will be no concession, no conciliation, no "+
        "finding the middle ground, and no give and take.";

        String tokens[]  =null;
```

```
      String splitPattern= "compromise|cooperate|concession|"+
      "conciliation|(finding the middle ground)|(give and take)";

      Pattern p = Pattern.compile(splitPattern);

      tokens=p.split(statement);

      System.out.println("REGEX PATTERN:\n"+splitPattern + "\n");

      System.out.println("STATEMENT:\n"+statement + "\n");


      System.out.println("TOKENS:");
      for (int i=0; i < tokens.length; i++){
      System.out.println(tokens[i]);
      }
   }
}
```

Output 2-1. Result of Running PatternSplit.java

```
C:\RegEx\code\chapter1>java Split
REGEX PATTERN:
compromise|cooperate|concession|conciliation|(finding the middle group)|(give
and take)

STATEMENT:
I will not compromise. I will not cooperate. There
will be no concession, no conciliation,
no finding the middle group, and no give and take.

TOKENS:
I will not
. I will not
. There will be no
, no
, no
, and no
.
```

You'll notice that Listing 2-5 uses the `Pattern.split` method, whereas Listing 1-12 uses the new `String.split` method. In effect, the two are identical because the `String.split` method simply defers to this method internally.

What you've done is really quite amazing and might have been ridiculously convoluted without regular expressions. You're actually using complicated artificial constructs—namely, English language synonyms—to decompose text. This isn't your father's J2SE.

> **NOTE** The `String` method further optimizes its search criteria by placing an invisible ^ before the pattern and a $ after it.

public String[] split(CharSequence input, int limit)

This method works in exactly the same way that `Pattern.split(CharSequence input)` does, except for one variation. The second parameter, `limit`, allows you to control how many elements are returned, as shown in the following sections.

Limit == 0

If you specify that the second parameter, `limit`, should equal 0, then this method behaves exactly like its overloaded counterpart. That is, it returns an array containing as many matching substrings as possible, and trailing spaces are discarded. Thus, the pattern

```
Pattern p = new Pattern.compile(",");
```

will return an array consisting of two elements when split against the candidate *Hello, Dolly*. An example of the usage of the method follows:

```
String tmp[] = p.split("Hello,Dolly", 0);
```

Similarly, `split` will return two elements when matched against the `String` *Hello, Dolly*, with a trailing comma character after the *y* in *Dolly*:

```
String tmp[] = p.split("Hello,Dolly,", 0);
```

However, you may not always want this behavior. For example, there may be a time when you want to limit the number of elements returned.

Limit > 0

Use a positive limit if you're interested in only a certain number of matches. You should use that number +1 as the limit. To split the String *Hello, Dolly, You, Are, My, Favorite* when you want only the first two tokens, use this:

```
String[] tmp = pattern.split("Hello, Dolly, You, Are, My, Favorite",3);
```

The value of the resulting String is as follows:

```
//tmp[0] is  "Hello",
// tmp[1] is "Dolly";
```

The interesting behavior here is that a third element is returned. In this case, the third element is

```
//tmp[2] is  "You, Are, My, Favorite";
```

Using a positive limit can potentially lead to performance enhancements, because the regex engine can stop searching when it meets the specified number of matches.

Limit < 0

Using a negative number—any negative number—for the limit tells the regex engine that you want to return as many matches as possible *and* that you want trailing spaces, if any, to be returned. Thus, for the regex pattern

```
Pattern p = Pattern.compile(",");
```

and the candidate String *Hello,Dolly*, the command

```
String tmp[] = p.split("Hello,Dolly", -1);
```

results in the following condition:

```
//tmp is equal to {"Hello","Dolly"};
```

However, for the String *Hello, Dolly,* with trailing spaces after the comma following *Dolly*, the method call

```
String tmp[] = p.split("Hello,Dolly,    ", -1);
```

results in this:

```
//tmp is equal to {"Hello","Dolly","     "};
```

Notice that the actual value of the negative limit doesn't matter, thus

```
p.split("Hello,Dolly", -1);
```

is exactly equivalent to this:

```
p.split("Hello,Dolly", -100);
```

The Matcher Object

Figure 2-2 illustrates the methods of the Matcher class. Please take a moment to study them.

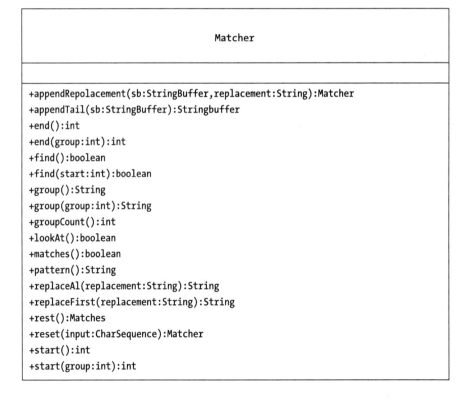

```
                              Matcher


+appendRepolacement(sb:StringBuffer,replacement:String):Matcher
+appendTail(sb:StringBuffer):Stringbuffer
+end():int
+end(group:int):int
+find():boolean
+find(start:int):boolean
+group():String
+group(group:int):String
+groupCount():int
+lookAt():boolean
+matches():boolean
+pattern():String
+replaceAl(replacement:String):String
+replaceFirst(replacement:String):String
+rest():Matches
+reset(input:CharSequence):Matcher
+start():int
+start(group:int):int
```

Figure 2-2. The Matcher class

The following sections describe the various methods of the `Matcher` class. But first, let's briefly revisit the concept of groups, as they figure so prominently in the `Matcher` object.

Groups

Before you can take full advantage of the `Matcher` object, it's important that you understand the concept of a *group*, as some of the more powerful methods of `Matcher` deal with them. I discuss groups in even greater detail in Chapter 3, but you need an intuitive sense of them to take full advantage of the material in this chapter, so I provide a brief introduction here.

A group is exactly what it sounds like: a cluster of characters. Often, the term refers to a subportion of the original `Pattern`, though each group is, by definition, a subgroup of itself. You're probably already familiar with the concept of groups from your study of arithmetic. For example, the expression

```
6 * 7 + 4
```

has an implicit sense of grouping. You really read it as

```
(6 * 7) + 4
```

where *(6 * 7)* is thought of as a clustering of numbers. Further, you can think of the expression as

```
( (6 * 7) + 4)
```

where you can consider *((6 * 7) + 4)* another clustering of numbers, this one including the subcluster *(6*7)*. Here, your group has a subgroup. Similarly, regex allows you to group a sequence of characters together. Why? I discuss that shortly. First, let's concentrate on how.

Remember that in regular expressions, you describe what you're looking for in general terms by using a `Pattern` object. Groups allow you to nest subdescriptions within your expression. As you examine a specific candidate `String`, the `Matcher` can keep track of submatches for that expression.

Creating a grouping of regex characters is very easy. You simply put the expression you want to think of as a group inside a pair of parentheses. That's it. Thus, the pattern *(\w)(\d\d)(\w+)* consists of four groups, ranging from 0 to 3. `group(0)`, which is always the original expression itself, is as follows:

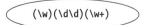

`(\w)(\d\d)(\w+)`

group(1), which consists of an alphanumeric or underscore character, is circled in the following image:

((\w))(\d\d)(\w+)

group(2) is circled in the following image:

(\w)((\d\d))(\w+)

group(3) is circled in the following image:

(\w)(\d\d)((\w+))

For a specific candidate String, say *X99SuperJava*, group(0) is always the part of the candidate string that matches the original regex pattern—namely, the pattern *(\w)(\d\d)(\w+)* itself:

X99SuperJava

The following image indicates the corresponding section of *X99SuperJava* for group(1):

X99SuperJava

The corresponding section of *X99SuperJava* for group(2) is circled in the following image:

X99SuperJava

The corresponding section of *X99SuperJava* for group(3) is circled in the following image:

X99SuperJava

OK, so you know how to designate groups and how to find the corresponding section in a candidate string. Now, why would you? A common reason for doing so is the ability to refer to subsections of the candidate string. For example, you may not know what this particular candidate string, namely *X99SuperJava*, is, but you can still write a program that rearranges it by creating a new String equal to group(3), appended to group(1), and appended to group(2). In this case, that rearranged String would be *SuperJavaX99*.

Chapter 3 provides detailed examples of groups.

public Pattern pattern()

The pattern method returns the Pattern that created this particular Matcher object. Consider Listing 2-6.

Listing 2-6. Matcher Pattern Example

```
import java.util.regex.*;

public class MatcherPatternExample{
  public static void main(String args[]){
      test();
  }

  public static void test(){
     Pattern p = Pattern.compile("\\d");
     Matcher m1 = p.matcher("55");
     Matcher m2 = p.matcher("fdshfdgdfh");

     System.out.println(m1.pattern() == m2.pattern());
     //return true
  }
}
```

You should notice a few important things here. First, both Matcher objects successfully returned a Pattern, even though m2 wasn't a successful match. Second, the Matcher objects returned *exactly the same* Pattern object, because they were both created by that Pattern. Notice that the line

```
System.out.println(m1.pattern() == m2.pattern());
```

did a == compare and not a .equals compare. This could only have worked if the actual object returned by m1 and m2 was, in fact, exactly the same object.

public Matcher reset()

The reset method clears all state information from the Matcher object it's called on. The Matcher is, in effect, reverted to the state it originally had when you first received a reference to it, as shown in Listing 2-7.

Listing 2-7. Matcher.reset Example

```java
import java.util.regex.*;
/**
 * Demonstrates the usage of the
 * Matcher.reset() method
 */
public class MatcherResetExample{
  public static void main(String args[]){
      test();
  }
  public static void test(){
     //create a pattern, and extract a matcher
     Pattern p = Pattern.compile("\\d");
     Matcher m1 = p.matcher("01234");

     //exhaust the matcher
     while (m1.find()){
      System.out.println("\t\t" + m1.group());
     }
     //now reset the matcher to its original state
     m1.reset();
     System.out.println("After resetting the Matcher");
     //iterate through the matcher again.
     //this would not be possible without a cleared state
     while (m1.find()){
      System.out.println("\t\t" + m1.group());
     }
  }
}
```

Output 2-2 shows the output of this method.

Output 2-2. Output for the Matcher.reset Example

```
        0
        1
        2
        3
        4
After resetting the Matcher
        0
        1
        2
        3
        4
```

You wouldn't have been able to iterate through the elements of the Matcher again if it hadn't been reset.

public Matcher reset(CharSequence input)

The reset(CharSequence input) methods clears the state of the Matcher object it's called on and replaces the candidate String with the new input. This has the same effect as creating a new Matcher object, except that it doesn't have as much of the associated overhead. This can lead to useful optimization, and it's one that I often use. Listing 2-8 demonstrates this method's usage.

Listing 2-8. Matcher.reset(CharSequence) Example

```java
import java.util.regex.*;
/**
 * Demonstrates the usage of the
 * Matcher.reset(CharSequence) method
 */
public class MatcherResetCharSequenceExample{
  public static void main(String args[]){
      test();
  }
```

```
public static void test(){
   String output="";
   //create a pattern, and extract a matcher
   Pattern p = Pattern.compile("\\d");
   Matcher m1 = p.matcher("01234");

   //exhaust the matcher
   while (m1.find()){
    System.out.println("\t\t" + m1.group());
   }
   //now reset the matcher with new data
   m1.reset("56789");
   System.out.println("After resetting the Matcher");
   //iterate through the matcher again.
   //this would not be possible without
   while (m1.find()){
    System.out.println("\t\t" + m1.group());
   }
 }
}
```

Output 2-3 shows the output of this method.

Output 2-3. Output for the Matcher.reset(CharSequence) Example

```
        0
        1
        2
        3
        4
After resetting the Matcher
        5
        6
        7
        8
        9
```

public int start()

The start method returns the starting index of the last successful match the
Matcher object had. Listing 2-9 demonstrates the use of the Start method. The
code in this listing finds the starting index of the word *Bond* in the candidate *My
name is Bond. James Bond..*

Listing 2-9. Matcher.start() Example

```
/**
 * Demonstrates the usage of the
 * Matcher.start() method
 */
public class MatcherStartExample{
  public static void main(String args[]){
      test();
  }
  public static void test(){
      //create a Matcher and use the Matcher.start() method
      String candidateString = "My name is Bond. James Bond.";
      String matchHelper[] =
        {"          ^","                    ^"};
      Pattern p = Pattern.compile("Bond");
      Matcher matcher = p.matcher(candidateString);

      //Find the starting point of the first 'Bond'
       matcher.find();
       int startIndex = matcher.start();
       System.out.println(candidateString);
       System.out.println(matchHelper[0] + startIndex);

      //Find the starting point of the second 'Bond'
       matcher.find();
       int nextIndex = matcher.start();
       System.out.println(candidateString);
       System.out.println(matchHelper[1] + nextIndex);
  }
```

Output 2-4 shows the output of running the start() method.

Output 2-4. Output for the Matcher.start() Example

```
My name is Bond. James Bond.
         ^11
My name is Bond. James Bond.
                     ^23
```

If you execute another `find()` method

```
matcher.find();
```

and then execute `start()`

```
int nonIndex = matcher.start(); //throws IllegalStateException
```

the `start()` method will throw an `IllegalStateException`. I'm surprised that it doesn't simply return a negative number to indicate an unsuccessful match. Use the boolean returned by the `matches()` method to determine whether you should call methods such as `start()`.

public int start(int group)

This method allows you to specify which subgroup within a match you're interested in. If there are no matches, or if no matches have been attempted, this method throws an `IllegalStateException`. Listing 2-10 demonstrates the use of the `start(int)` method shortly. But before examining the code, let's take a step back and consider what the code is actually trying to demonstrate.

In the following example, the regex pattern is *B(ond)*, which means that you have a subgroup within the pattern (the parentheses indicate a subgroup). The following is the portion of the candidate parsed when `find()` is called for the first time:

```
My name is Bond. James Bond.
```

Thus, when you call the `start(0)` method, you're implicitly calling it only for the region that has already been parsed, which is outlined in the box. As far as the `Matcher` is concerned, this boxed region is the only one we can currently discuss. This is simply the nature of the `find` method, and it has nothing to do with the `start(int)` method yet.

The start(0) method returns the index of the first character in group(0), which is the *B* in *Bond*. group(0) is circled in the following image.

```
My name is (Bond). James Bond.
```

Similarly, when you call start(1), you're calling it only for the region that has already been parsed—again, the boxed region in the preceding image. This time, you're asking for the second grouping in the parsed region. The start(1) method returns the index of the first character in group(1), which is the *o* in *Bond*. group(1) is circled in the following image:

```
My name is B(ond). James Bond.
```

Next, you call matcher.find() again, which results in a new region of the candidate string coming under consideration, as shown in the following image:

```
My name is Bond. James Bond.
```

Calling the start(0) method here implicitly calls it only for the new region that has already been parsed, which appears in the box in the preceding image. This is the only region the associated Matcher will consider. start(0) returns the index of first character in group(0), which is the *B* in *Bond*. group(0) is circled in the following image:

```
My name is Bond. James (Bond).
```

Again, calling start(1) asks the Matcher to consider only the new region that has been parsed—again, the boxed region. This time, you're asking for the second grouping in the parsed region. start(1) returns the index of first character in group(1), which is the *o* in *Bond*. group(1) is circled in the boxed region.

```
My name is Bond. James B(ond.)
```

When you consider the process visually, it's easy to understand how the start(int) method interacts with groups, group numbers, and the find() method. find() parses just enough of the candidate string for all groups to match and works in that limited region. Keep this in mind as you read through Listing 2-10. Listing 2-10 is a fully working example of the algorithm discussed in this section. Please refer back to the preceding images as necessary when you read the example.

Listing 2-10. Matcher.start(int) Example

```java
import java.util.regex.*;
/**
 * Demonstrates the usage of the
 * Matcher.start(int) method
 */
public class MatcherStartParamExample{
  public static void main(String args[]){
      test();
  }
  public static void test(){
     //create a Pattern
      Pattern p = Pattern.compile("B(ond)");

     //create a Matcher and use the Matcher.start(int) method
     String candidateString = "My name is Bond. James Bond.";
     //create a helpful index for the sake of output
     String matchHelper[] =
                               {"          ^",
                                "             ^",
                                "                        ^",
                                "                         ^"};
     Matcher matcher = p.matcher(candidateString);
     //Find the starting point of the first 'B(ond)'
      matcher.find();
      int startIndex = matcher.start(0);
      System.out.println(candidateString);
      System.out.println(matchHelper[0] + startIndex);

     //find the starting point of the first subgroup (ond)
     int nextIndex = matcher.start(1);
     System.out.println(candidateString);
     System.out.println(matchHelper[1] + nextIndex);

     //Find the starting point of the second 'B(ond)'
      matcher.find();
      startIndex = matcher.start(0);
      System.out.println(candidateString);
      System.out.println(matchHelper[2] + startIndex);
```

```
    //find the starting point of the second subgroup (ond)
    nextIndex = matcher.start(1);
    System.out.println(candidateString);
    System.out.println(matchHelper[3] + nextIndex);
  }
}
```

Output 2-5 shows the output of running the start() method.

Output 2-5. Output for the Matcher.start(int) Example

```
My name is Bond. James Bond.
           ^11
My name is Bond. James Bond.
           ^12
My name is Bond. James Bond.
                      ^23
My name is Bond. James Bond.
                       ^24
```

If you execute another find() method

```
matcher.find();
```

and then execute start()

```
int nonIndex = matcher.start(0); //throws IllegalStateException
```

the start(int) method will throw an IllegalStateException because the find() method wasn't successful. Similarly, it will throw an IndexOutOfBoundsException if you try to refer to a group number that doesn't exist.

public int end()

The end method returns the ending index of the last successful match the Matcher object had plus 1. If no matches exist, or if no matches have been attempted, this method throws an IllegalStateException. Listing 2-11 demonstrates the use of the end method.

Listing 2-11. Matcher.end() Example

```
/**
 * Demonstrates the usage of the
 * Matcher.end() method
 */
public class MatcherEndExample{
  public static void main(String args[]){
      test();
  }
  public static void test(){
     //create a Matcher and use the Matcher.end() method
     String candidateString = "My name is Bond. James Bond.";
     String matchHelper[] =
       {"                  ^"," ^"};
     Pattern p = Pattern.compile("Bond");
     Matcher matcher = p.matcher(candidateString);

     //Find the end point of the first 'Bond'
      matcher.find();
      int endIndex= matcher.end();
      System.out.println(candidateString);
      System.out.println(matchHelper[0] + endIndex);

     //Find the end point of the second 'Bond'
      matcher.find();
      int nextIndex = matcher.end();
      System.out.println(candidateString);
      System.out.println(matchHelper[1] + nextIndex);
  }
}
```

Output 2-6 shows the output of running the end method.

Output 2-6. Output for the Matcher.end() Example

```
My name is Bond. James Bond.
               ^15
My name is Bond. James Bond.
                        ^27
```

If you execute another `find` method

```
matcher.find();
```

and then execute `end`

```
int nonIndex = matcher.end(); //throws IllegalStateException
```

the `end` method will throw an `IllegalStateException`, because there isn't a valid group to find the end of.

public int end(int group)

Like the `start(int)` method, this method allows you to specify which subgroup within a matching you're interested in. It returns the last index of the matching character sequence plus 1. Listing 2-12 demonstrates the usage of the `end(int)` method shortly.

In the following example, the regex pattern is *B(on)d*, which means you have a subgroup within the pattern. The area that has been examined by the `Matcher` after `find()` is initially called is highlighted in the box shown in the following image:

```
My name is Bond. James Bond.
```

By calling the `end(0)` method, you're implicitly calling it only for the region that has already been parsed, which is boxed in the preceding image. As far as the `Matcher` is currently concerned, this boxed region is the only one we can discuss at present.

The `end(0)` method returns the index of last character in `group(0)` plus 1. Remember that `group(0)` is the entire expression *B(on)d*. In this region, the last character is the *d* in *Bond*, which is at position 14. Because `end(int)` adds 1 to that last index, 15 is returned. `group(0)` is circled in the following image:

```
My name is Bond. James Bond.
```

Similarly, when you call `end(1)`, you're calling it only for the region that has already been parsed—again, the boxed region. This time, you're asking for the second grouping in that region. The `end(1)` method returns the index of the last character in `group(1)` plus 1. The last character in `group(1)` is the *n* in *Bond*, because the pattern is *B(on)d*, and the index of that *n* is 13. Because `end` adds 1 to the index, 14 is returned. `group(1)` is circled in the following image:

```
My name is Bond. James Bond.
```

Next, you call matcher.find() again, which results in a new region of the candidate String coming under consideration, as shown here:

My name is Bond. James Bond.

Calling the end(0) method implicitly calls it only for the new region that has already been parsed, which is boxed in the preceding image. The end(0) method returns the index of last character in group(0) plus 1, which is the *d* in *Bond*. The index of *d* is 26, and because end adds 1 to that number, 27 is returned. group(0) is circled in the following image:

My name is Bond. James Bond.

Calling end(1) only considers the new region that been parsed—again, the boxed region. This time, you're asking for the second grouping in the parsed region. The end(1) method returns the index of last character in group(1) plus 1. That last character is the *o* in *Bond*, which is at index 25, as shown in the following image. Because end(int) adds 1 to that number, 26 in returned. The result of calling group(1) is as follows:

My name is Bond. James Bond.

Please refer back to the preceding images as necessary when you read Listing 2-12. The listing is simply a fully working example of the steps you just went through.

Listing 2-12. Matcher.end(int) Example

```java
import java.util.regex.*;
/**
 * Demonstrates the usage of the
 * Matcher.end(int) method
 */
public class MatcherEndParamExample{
  public static void main(String args[]){
      test();
  }
  public static void test(){
     //create a Pattern
      Pattern p = Pattern.compile("B(on)d");
```

```
//create a Matcher and use the Matcher.start(int) method
String candidateString = "My name is Bond. James Bond.";
//create a helpful index for the sake of output
String matchHelper[] =
                              {"                    ^",
                               "                    ^",
                               "                           ^",
                               "                           ^"};
Matcher matcher = p.matcher(candidateString);
//Find the end point of the first 'B(ond)'
 matcher.find();
 int endIndex = matcher.end(0);
 System.out.println(candidateString);
 System.out.println(matchHelper[0] + endIndex);

 //find the end point of the first subgroup (ond)
 int nextIndex = matcher.end(1);
 System.out.println(candidateString);
 System.out.println(matchHelper[1] + nextIndex);

//Find the end point of the second 'B(ond)'
 matcher.find();
 endIndex = matcher.end(0);
 System.out.println(candidateString);
 System.out.println(matchHelper[2] + endIndex);

 //find the end point of the second subgroup (ond)
 nextIndex = matcher.end(1);
 System.out.println(candidateString);
 System.out.println(matchHelper[3] + nextIndex);
  }
}
```

Output 2-7 shows the output of running Listing 2-12.

Output 2-7. Output for the Matcher.end(int) Example

```
My name is Bond. James Bond.
              ^15
My name is Bond. James Bond.
            ^14
My name is Bond. James Bond.
                        ^27
My name is Bond. James Bond.
                      ^26
```

If you execute another `find()` method

```
matcher.find();
```

and then execute `end()`

```
int nonIndex = matcher.end(0); //throws IllegalStateException
```

the `end(int)` method will throw an `IllegalStateException` if the `find` method isn't successful or if it isn't called in the first place. Similarly, it will throw an `IndexOutOfBoundsException` if you try to refer to a group number that doesn't exist.

public String group()

The group method can be a powerful and convenient tool in the war against jumbled code. It simply returns the substring of the candidate `String` that matches the original regex pattern. For example, say you want to extract occurrences of the pattern ***Bond***

```
Pattern p = Pattern.compile("Bond");
```

from the candidate `String` *My name is Bond. James Bond.*. You extract the `Matcher`

```
Matcher matcher = p.matches("My name is Bond. James Bond.");
```

and call `find()` on it.

```
Matcher.find();
```

Now the boxed region in the following image is ready to be scrutinized by the `Matcher`:

My name is Bond. James Bond.

You can now extract the part of the candidate `String` that matches your criteria by using the group() method:

```
String tmp = matcher.group(); \\return "Bond";
```

This method extracts the matching part of the region under consideration. That area is circled in the following image:

My name is (Bond). James Bond.

A clumsier way of achieving the same result is to use the `start` and `end` methods to find the starting and ending indexes of the group within the candidate `String`, and use a `String.substring` method to extract that text.

The group() method will throw an `IllegalStateException` if the find() method is unsuccessful or if it's never initially called. Listing 2-13 presents a complete working example of this method and the algorithm discussed.

Listing 2-13. The Matcher.group() Method

```
import java.util.regex.*;
/**
 * Demonstrates the usage of the
 * Matcher.group() method
 */
public class MatcherGroupExample{
  public static void main(String args[]){
      test();
  }
  public static void test(){
      //create a Pattern
      Pattern p = Pattern.compile("Bond");

      //create a Matcher and use the Matcher.group() method
      String candidateString = "My name is Bond. James Bond.";
      Matcher matcher = p.matcher(candidateString);
      //extract the group
      matcher.find();
      System.out.println(matcher.group());
  }
}
```

public String group(int group)

This method is a more powerful counterpart to the group() method. It allows you to extract parts of a candidate String that match a subgroup within your pattern. The use of the group(int) method is demonstrated shortly in Listing 2-14.

In the following example, the regex pattern is again *B(ond)*, which means you have a subgroup within the pattern. The portion the candidate parsed when find() is called for the first time is shown here:

```
My name is Bond. James Bond.
```

Thus, when you call the group(0) method, you're implicitly calling it only for the region that has already been parsed, which is boxed in the preceding image. As far as the Matcher is currently concerned, this boxed region is the only one we can discuss.

Calling group(0) returns *Bond* because that's the first group that matches your criteria in the region of the candidate String currently under inspection. Again, that area is shown in the box in the preceding image. The actual matching group is shown in the following image:

```
My name is (Bond). James Bond.
```

Similarly, when you call group(1), you're calling it only for the region that has already been parsed—again, the boxed area. This time, you're asking for the second grouping in the parsed region. group(1) is circled in the following image:

```
My name is B(ond). James Bond.
```

Next, you call matcher.find() again, which results in a new region of the candidate String coming under inspection, as shown here:

```
My name is Bond. James Bond.
```

Calling the group(0) method implicitly calls it only for the new region that has already been parsed, which is boxed in the preceding image. The group(0) method returns the String *Bond*. group(0) is circled in the following image:

```
My name is Bond. James (Bond).
```

Calling group(1) only considers the new region that been parsed—again, the boxed region. Within that region, group(1) refers to *ond*. group(1) is circled in the following image:

```
My name is Bond. James B(ond.)
```

Listing 2-14 presents an example using the group(int) method, and Output 2-8 shows the output of this example.

Listing 2-14. Matcher.group(int) Method Example

```
import java.util.regex.*;
/**
 * Demonstrates the usage of the
 * Matcher.group(int) method
 */
public class MatcherGroupParamExample{
  public static void main(String args[]){
      test();
  }
  public static void test(){
     //create a Pattern
      Pattern p = Pattern.compile("B(ond)");

     //create a Matcher and use the Matcher.group(int) method
     String candidateString = "My name is Bond. James Bond.";
     //create a helpful index for the sake of output
     Matcher matcher = p.matcher(candidateString);
     //Find group number 0 of the first find
      matcher.find();
      String group_0 = matcher.group(0);
      String group_1 = matcher.group(1);
      System.out.println("Group 0 " + group_0);
      System.out.println("Group 1 " + group_1);
      System.out.println(candidateString);

     //Find group number 1 of the second find
      matcher.find();
      group_0 = matcher.group(0);
      group_1 = matcher.group(1);
      System.out.println("Group 0 " + group_0);
      System.out.println("Group 1 " + group_1);
      System.out.println(candidateString);
  }
}
```

Output 2-8. Output of the Matcher.Group(int) Example

```
My name is Bond. James Bond.
Group 0 Bond
Group 1 ond
My name is Bond. James Bond.
Group 0 Bond
Group 1 ond
```

If you execute another `find()` method

```
matcher.find();
```

and then execute group(0)

```
String tmp = matcher.group(0); //throws IllegalStateException
```

the group(0) method will throw an IllegalStateException because the find method call wasn't successful. Similarly, it will throw an IllegalStateException if find hadn't been called at all. If you try to refer to a group number that doesn't exist, it will throw an IndexOutOfBoundsException.

public int groupCount()

This method simply returns the number of groups that the Pattern defined. In Listing 2-15, the groupCount method displays the number of possible groups a given pattern might have.

Listing 2-15. MatcherGroupCountExample Example

```
import java.util.regex.*;
/**
 * Demonstrates the usage of the
 * Matcher.groupCount() method
 */
public class MatcherGroupCountExample{
  public static void main(String args[]){
      test();
  }
```

```java
public static void test(){
    //create a Pattern
    Pattern p = Pattern.compile("B(ond)");

    //create a Matcher and use the Matcher.group() method
    String candidateString = "My name is Bond. James Bond.";
    Matcher matcher = p.matcher(candidateString);

    //extract the possible number of groups.
    //It's important to be aware that this
    //represents only the number of groups that
    //are possible: not the actual number of groups
    //found in the candidate string
    int numberOfGroups = matcher.groupCount();
    System.out.println("numberOfGroups ="+numberOfGroups);
    }
}
```

There's a very important, and somewhat counterintuitive, subtlety to notice about this method. It returns the number of possible groups based on the original Pattern, without even considering the candidate String. Thus, it's not really information about the Matcher object; rather, it's information about the Pattern that helped spawn it. This can be tricky, because the fact that this method lives on the Matcher object could be interpreted to mean that it's providing feedback about the state of the Matcher. It just isn't. It's telling you how many matches are theoretically possible for the given Pattern.

public boolean matches()

This method is designed to help you match a candidate String against the Matcher's Pattern. If it returns true if—and only if—the candidate String under consideration matches the pattern exactly.

Listing 2-16 demonstrates how you might use this method. Three strings, *j2se*, *J2SE*, and *J2SE* (notice the space after the *E*), are compared to the Pattern *J2SE*.

Listing 2-16. Matcher.matches Example

```
    import java.util.regex.*;
/**
 * Demonstrates the usage of the
 * Matcher.matches method
 */
public class MatcherMatchesExample{
  public static void main(String args[]){
      test();
  }
  public static void test(){
     //create a Pattern
      Pattern p = Pattern.compile("J2SE");

     //create the candidate Strings
     String candidateString_1 = "j2se";
     String candidateString_2 = "J2SE ";
     String candidateString_3 = "J2SE";

     //Attempt to match the candidate Strings.
     Matcher matcher_1 = p.matcher(candidateString_1);
     Matcher matcher_2 = p.matcher(candidateString_2);
     Matcher matcher_3 = p.matcher(candidateString_3);

     //display the output for first candidate
     String msg = ":" + candidateString_1 + ": matches?: ";
     System.out.println( msg + matcher_1.matches());

     //display the output for second candidate
     msg = ":" + candidateString_2 + ": matches?: ";
     System.out.println(msg + matcher_2.matches());

     //display the output for third candidate
     msg = ":" + candidateString_3 + ": matches?: ";
     System.out.println(msg + matcher_3.matches());
  }
}
```

Only one of the three candidates successfully matches here. *j2se* is rejected because it is the wrong case. *J2SE* is again rejected because it contains a space character after the *E*, which means that it isn't a perfect match. The only perfect match is *J2SE*.

public boolean find()

The find() method parses just enough of the candidate string to find a match. If such a substring is successfully found, then true is returned and find stops parsing the candidate. If no part of the candidate string matches the pattern, then find returns false.

Thus, for the pattern

```
Pattern p = Pattern.compile("Bond");
```

and candidate String *My name is Bond. James Bond.*

```
Matcher matcher = p.matcher("My name is Bond. James Bond");
```

calling find() parses *My name is Bond. James Bond.* until the substring *My name is Bond* meets the first *Bond*, as follows:

My name is Bond. James Bond.

The boxed section is the part of the candidate that has been parsed; thus, it's the part that calls to the start, end, or group methods we will be concerned with. Why? Because the find method only had to parse up to *d* in *Bond* to find a match. Having accomplished that mission, the find method doesn't waste resources parsing the rest of the candidate String.

Calling find is a necessary preamble to using methods such as start, end, and group. Without first evoking find, calling these methods will cause an IllegalStateException to be thrown.

One common use of this method is as a control condition in a while loop, so that the start, end, or group method isn't called when they might throw an IllegalStateException. Listing 2-17 is an example of a simple regular expression that loops through the String *I love Java. Java is my favorite language. Java Java Java.* and finds the pattern ***Java***.

Listing 2-17. Using the find() Method

```
import java.util.regex.*;
/**
 * Demonstrates the usage of the
 * Matcher.find method
 */
public class MatcherFindExample{
  public static void main(String args[]){
      test();
  }
```

```java
public static void test(){
    //create a Pattern
     Pattern p = Pattern.compile("Java");

    //create the candidate String
    String candidateString =
     "I love Java. Java is my favorite language. Java Java Java.";

    //Attempt to match the candidate String.
    Matcher matcher = p.matcher(candidateString);

    //loop through and display all matches
    while (matcher.find()){
       System.out.println(matcher.group());
    }
  }
}
```

In this example, the candidate String is

```java
String candidateString =
 "I love Java. Java is my favorite language. Java Java Java.";
```

When the while loop is fist entered, find() is immediately called on the Matcher, which results in the boxed area in the following image. Within that boxed region, the matching part of the region is circled, as shown in the images that follow.

The boxed area is the region parsed, and the circled part is the matching substring:

I love Java. Java is my favorite language. Java Java Java.

The boxed area is the next region parsed, and the circled part is the matching substring:

I love Java. Java is my favorite language. Java Java Java.

The boxed area is the next region parsed, and the circled part is the matching substring:

I love Java. Java is my favorite language. Java Java Java.

The boxed area is the next region parsed, and the circled part is the matching substring:

I love Java. Java is my favorite language. Java Java Java.

The boxed area is the next region parsed, and the circled part is the matching substring:

```
I love Java. Java is my favorite language. Java Java Java.
```

public boolean find(int start)

The find(int start) method works exactly like its overloaded counterpart, except for where it starts searching. The int parameter in start simply tells the Matcher at which character to start its search on.

Thus, for the candidate String *I love Java. Java is my favorite language. Java Java Java.* and the pattern **Java**, if you only want to start searching at character index 11, you use the command find(11). The area parsed is boxed in the following image, and the actual matching group is circled:

```
I love Java. Java is my favorite language. Java Java Java.
```

If the index given is greater than the length of the candidate string, then this method will throw an IndexOutOfBoundsException. Thus, for the preceding candidate string, calling find(58) will cause an IndexOutOfBoundsException, because the length of the string is only 57.

You can also use this method to set the start of the searching point. Thus, you could execute find(11) to start searching at character 11, and then use find(0) to start searching at character 0.

Listing 2-18 provides an example for the candidate String *I hate mice. I really hate MICE.* and the pattern **MICE**, in which the comparison is made is case insensitive. The code uses a case-insensitive comparison to demonstrate that the first match is, in fact, for the String that matches after character number 11.

Listing 2-18. Using the find(int) Method

```java
import java.util.regex.*;
/**
 * Demonstrates the usage of the
 * Matcher.find(int) method
 */
public class MatcherFindParamExample{
  public static void main(String args[]){
      test();
  }
}
```

```
public static void test(){
   //create a Pattern
    Pattern p = Pattern.compile("mice", Pattern.CASE_INSENSITIVE);

   //create the candidate String
   String candidateString =
    "I hate mice. I really hate MICE.";

   //Attempt to match the candidate String.
   Matcher matcher = p.matcher(candidateString);

   //display the latter match
   System.out.println(candidateString);
   matcher.find(11);
   System.out.println(matcher.group());

   //display the earlier match
   System.out.println(candidateString);
   matcher.find(0);
   System.out.println(matcher.group());
 }
}
```

When you execute the find(11) method, the search region starts character 11, as illustrated in the following image:

```
I hate mice. I really hate MICE.
```

Next, you execute find(0), which moves the search index back to 0. The following image illustrates the resulting search region:

```
I hate mice. I really hate MICE.
```

public boolean lookingAt()

The lookingAt() method is a more relaxed version of the matches method. It simply compares as little of the String against the Pattern as necessary to achieve a match. If such a subsection exists, then this method returns true.

Thus, for the pattern *J2SE*

```
Pattern = Pattern.compile("J2SE");
```

and the candidate *J2SE is the only one for me*

```
Matcher matcher_1 = Pattern.matcher("J2SE is the only one for me");
```

the `lookingAt` method returns true. However, calling `lookingAt()` for the candidate string *For me, it's J2SE, or nothing at all*

```
Matcher matcher_2 = Pattern.matcher("For me, it's J2SE, or nothing at all");
```

will return false, because the first part of *For me, it's J2SE, or nothing at all* doesn't match the pattern *J2SE*.

Like the `matches` method, the `lookingAt` method always starts looking at the candidate string at the beginning of the input sequence; unlike `matches`, the `lookingAt` method doesn't require that the entire input sequence be matched. If the match succeeds, then more information can be obtained by using the `start`, `end`, and `group` methods. Listing 2-19 provides an example of the `lookingAt` method's use.

Listing 2-19. Using the lookingAt Method

```
import java.util.regex.*;
/**
 * Demonstrates the usage of the
 * Matcher.LookingAt method
 */
public class MatcherLookingAtExample{
  public static void main(String args[]){
      test();
  }
  public static void test(){
     //create a Pattern
      Pattern p = Pattern.compile("J2SE");

     //create the candidate Strings
     String candidateString_1 = "J2SE is the only one for me";
     String candidateString_2 =
       "For me, it's J2SE, or nothing at all";
     String candidateString_3 = "J2SEistheonlyoneforme";

     //Attempt to match the candidate Strings.
     Matcher matcher = p.matcher(candidateString_1);
     //display the output for the candidate
     String msg = ":" + candidateString_1 + ": matches?: ";
     System.out.println( msg + matcher.lookingAt());
```

```
        matcher.reset(candidateString_2);
        //display the output for the candidates
        msg = ":" + candidateString_2 + ": matches?: ";
        System.out.println( msg + matcher.lookingAt());

        matcher.reset(candidateString_3);
        //display the output for the candidate
        msg = ":" + candidateString_3 + ": matches?: ";
        System.out.println( msg + matcher.lookingAt());

        /*
        *returns
        *:J2SE is the only one for me: matches?: true
        *:For me, it's J2SE, or nothing at all: matches?: false
        *:J2SEistheonlyoneforme: matches?: true
        */
    }
}
```

public Matcher appendReplacement (StringBuffer sb, String replacement)

There will be times when you'll prefer to use a StringBuffer instead of a String when working with regular expressions. This might be for performance, utility, or other reasons. Fortunately, the java.util.regex package offers the appendReplacement and appendTail methods for doing so. This section focuses on the appendReplacement method.

Simply speaking, appendReplacement allows you to create a StringBuffer based on the contents of your Pattern and Matcher objects. Say you want to swap out *Smith* for *Bond* in the *My name is Bond. James Bond. I would like a martini.*, and you want the results stored in a StringBuffer. To use appendReplacement, you must first create a Pattern and a corresponding Matcher. For this example's purposes, you'll use **Bond**:

```
Pattern pattern = Pattern.compile("Bond");
```

Also, you'll work with the candidate string *My name is Bond. James Bond. I would like a martini.*:

```
Matcher matcher =
 pattern.matcher("My name is Bond. James Bond. I would like a martini.");
```

Next, you call the find method, so that the Matcher can start to parse the candidate String. The first time you call find, the Matcher simply parses enough of the candidate String such that the first match, if any, is found. This parsed region is boxed in the following image:

My name is Bond. James Bond. I would like a martini.

Recall that the boxed region is the only part of the candidate string the Matcher is currently aware of.

Then you'll call the appendReplacement method, which populates the StringBuffer sb with everything in the boxed region shown in the preceding image, except that *Smith* is swapped out for *Bond*. Therefore, your StringBuffer now contains *My name is Smith*.

One last thing bears mentioning. Internally, the Matcher object maintains an *append position*. This append position is state information maintained by the Matcher object for the sake of the StringBuffer object. It records the position in the StringBuffer that the last call to appendReplacement read from. Of course, the append position is initially 0, as shown in the following image:

My name is Bond. James Bond. I would like a martini.

Append Position

After you call appendReplacement, the append position is moved forward to just after the match, as shown in the following image. This is the same position that the matcher.end() method would return.

My name is Bond. James Bond. I would like a martini.

Append Position

Next, you call matcher.find() again, so that the current position under consideration becomes the boxed region highlighted in the following image:

My name is Bond. James Bond. I would like a martini.

Append Position

You then call appendReplacement again, thus appending . *James Smith* to the StringBuffer. Remember, because this is a replacement method, it automatically replaces *Bond* with *Smith*. The content of the StringBuffer becomes *My name is Smith. James Smith*, and the append position is moved forward, as shown in the following image:

```
My name is Bond. James Bond.  I would like a martini.
                          ↑
                    Append Position
```

Your mission is accomplished. The complete code listing is displayed in Listing 2-20.

Listing 2-20. appendReplacement Method Example

```java
import java.util.regex.*;
import java.util.*;
/**
 * Demonstrates usage of the
 * Matcher.appendReplacement method
 */
public class Scrap{
  public static void main(String args[]){
      test();
  }
  public static void test(){
     //create a Pattern
      Pattern p = Pattern.compile("Bond");
      //create a StringBuffer
      StringBuffer sb =new StringBuffer();

     //create the candidate Strings
     String candidateString =
     "My name is Bond. James Bond. I would like a martini.";

     String replacement = "Smith";
     //Attempt to match the first candidate String
     Matcher matcher = p.matcher(candidateString);
     matcher.find();

     //populate the StringBufffer
     matcher.appendReplacement(sb,replacement);
```

```
        //Attempt to match the second candidate String
        Matcher matcher = p.matcher(candidateString);
        matcher.find();

        //populate the StringBufffer
        matcher.appendReplacement(sb,replacement);

        //display the output for the candidate
        String msg = sb.toString();

        System.out.println(msg.length());
        System.out.println( msg );
    }
}
```

Special Notes

This appendReplacement method offers a lot of power. As you may know, with great power comes subtle distinctions. By using the expression *$d*, in which *d* is a number less than or equal to the number of groups in the previous match, you can actually embed and reorganize subgroups in your search. For example, say your pattern is *(James) (Bond)*:

```
        Pattern p = Pattern.compile("(James) (Bond)");
```

and your candidate is *My name is Bond. James Bond.*

```
        String candidateString = "My name is Bond. James Bond.";
```

and you want to insert the middle name *Waldo*. Your replacement String might look like the following:

```
String replacement = "$1 Waldo $2";
```

where *$1* refers to the first matching subgroup, *James*, and *$2* refers to the second matching subgroup, *Bond*.

In this case, the StringBuffer will contain the value *My name is Bond. James Waldo Bond.*. Listing 2-20 presents a complete working example.

Listing 2-20. Using appendReplacement with Subgroup Replacements

```java
import java.util.regex.*;
import java.ulil.*;
/**
 * Demonstrates usage of the
 * Matcher.appendReplacement method, with
 * subgroup replacement.
 */
public class MatcherAppendReplacementGroupExample{
  public static void main(String args[]){
      test();
  }
  public static void test(){
     //create a Pattern
      Pattern p = Pattern.compile("(James) (Bond)");
      //create a StringBuffer
      StringBuffer sb =new StringBuffer();

     //create the candidate Strings
     String candidateString =
     "My name is Bond. James Bond.";

     String replacement = "$1 Waldo $2";
     //Attempt to match the first candidate String
     Matcher matcher = p.matcher(candidateString);
     matcher.find();

     //populate the StringBufffer
     matcher.appendReplacement(sb,replacement);

     //display the output for the candidate
     String msg = sb.toString();
     System.out.println( msg );
  }
}
```

The appendReplacement method will throw an IllegalStateException if a find() has not been called, or if find returns false. It will throw an IndexOutOfBoundsException if the capturing group referred to by *$1*, *$2*, and so on doesn't exist in the part of the pattern currently being scrutinized by the Matcher.

public StringBuffer appendTail(StringBuffer sb)

The appendTail method is a supplement to the appendReplacement method. It simply appends every remaining subsequence from the original candidate string to the StringBuffer. It reads from the append position, which I explained in the appendReplacement section, to the end of the candidate string.

In the appendReplacement example given earlier, you swapped out *Smith* for *Bond* in the string *My name is Bond. James Bond. I would like a martini.*. When you finished, you had a StringBuffer that contained the value *My name is Smith. James Smith*.

That was as much as the appendReplacement method could accomplish for you, because it's based on a successful match, and there are no more successful matches to be found after the *d* in the second occurrence of the word *Bond*. The state of the Matcher after the second call to appendReplacement is shown in the following image:

```
My name is Bond. James Bond.  I would like a martini.
```

Append Position

Correspondingly, the StringBuffer created by using appendReplacement would only have contained the phrase *My name is Smith. James Smith*. The appendTail method simply appends the rest of the String, namely *. I would like a martini*. to the StringBuffer buffer. That same StringBuffer is returned.

public String replaceAll(String replacement)

This method is one of my favorite new additions, both for its functionality and for its intuitive application programming interface (API). The replaceAll method simply returns a String that replaces every occurrence of the description with the replacement.

Imagine that you have the String *I love ice. Ice is my favorite. Ice Ice Ice.*, and you want to replace every occurrence of *ice* or *Ice* with the word *Java*. Your first step is to describe the word you want to look for. In this case, because you want to match both uppercase *Ice* and lowercase *ice* you'll use the regex pattern *(i|I)ce*:

```
Pattern pattern = Pattern.compile("(i|I)ce");
```

Next, use the candidate String to get a Matcher:

```
Matcher matcher = pattern.matcher("I love ice. Ice is my favorite. Ice Ice Ice.");
```

Finally, make the replacement:

```
String tmp = matcher.replaceAll("Java");
```

Now the string tmp holds the value *I love Java. Java is my favorite. Java Java Java.*. Listing 2-21 presents the complete code for this example.

Listing 2-21. replaceAll Method Example

```
import java.util.regex.*;
import java.util.*;
/**
 * Demonstrates usage of the
 * Matcher.replaceAll method
 */
public class MatcherReplaceAllExample{
  public static void main(String args[]){
      test();
  }
  public static void test(){
     //create a Pattern
      Pattern p = Pattern.compile("(i|I)ce");

     //create the candidate String
     String candidateString =
     "I love ice. Ice is my favorite. Ice Ice Ice.";

     Matcher matcher = p.matcher(candidateString);
     String tmp = matcher.replaceAll("Java");

     System.out.println( tmp );
  }
}
```

> **CAUTION**   Using this method will change the state of your Matcher object.
> Specifically, the reset method will be called. Therefore, it's as if all start, end,
> group, and find calls hadn't been called.

Like the `appendReplacement` method, this `replaceAll` method can contain references to substrings by using the *$* symbol. For details, please see the `appendReplacement` documentation presented earlier in the chapter.

public String replaceFirst(String replacement)

The `replaceFirst` method is a more focused version of the `replaceAll` method. This method returns a `String` that replaces the *first* occurrence of the description with the replacement.

Imagine that you have the candidate *I love ice. Ice is my favorite. Ice Ice Ice.*, and you want to replace the first occurrence of *ice* or *Ice* with the word *Java*. Again, your first step is to describe the word you want to look for. In this case, because you want to match both uppercase *Ice* and lowercase *ice*, you use the regex pattern *(i|I)ce*:

```
Pattern pattern = Pattern.compile("(i|I)ce");
```

Next, use the candidate `String` to get a `Matcher`:

```
Matcher matcher = pattern.matcher("I love ice. Ice is my favorite. Ice Ice Ice.");
```

Finally, make the replacement:

```
String tmp = matcher.replaceFirst("Java");
```

The string `tmp` holds the value *I love Java. Ice is my favorite. Ice Ice Ice.*. Listing 2-22 presents the complete code for this example.

Listing 2-22. replaceFirst Method Example

```
import java.util.regex.*;
import java.util.*;
/**
 * Demonstrates usage of the
 * Matcher.replaceFirst method
 */
public class MatcherReplaceFirstExample{
  public static void main(String args[]){
      test();
  }
```

```
public static void test(){
   //create a Pattern
    Pattern p = Pattern.compile("(i|I)ce");

   //create the candidate String
   String candidateString =
   "I love ice. Ice is my favorite. Ice Ice Ice.";

   Matcher matcher = p.matcher(candidateString);
   String tmp = matcher.replaceFirst("Java");

   System.out.println( tmp );
}}
```

> **CAUTION** Using this method will change the state of your Matcher object. Specifically, the reset method will be called. Therefore, remember that all start, end, group, and find calls will have to be re-executed.

Like the appendReplacement method, the replaceFirst method can contain references to substring by using the $ symbol. For details, please see the appendReplacement documentation presented earlier in the chapter.

New String Rejex-Friendly Methods

One of the most obvious changes brought about by the introduction of regular expressions into J2SE is the addition of five powerful new methods in the String class. In the following sections I discuss these changes and offer direction on how you can use them in your future coding adventures.

The Art of Delimiting Strings

There's one very important consideration that you have to keep in mind when you work with regular expressions and String objects: Special characters, such as the digit, \d, and the word token, \w, to name just a couple, have to be delimited twice when passed into a String. For example, to search for a digit, you must double the number of \ characters you use. Thus, \d becomes \\d when you use it in a Java String object.

This doesn't sound overly complicated, but it can be surprisingly difficult to deal with at times. For example, imagine that you want to replace every occurrence of the character *d* in *I want to use a d character* with *d*. That is, you want the new String to say *I want to use a \d character*. How do you start?

Of course, you could try this:

```
String retval = tmp.replaceAll("d","\d");
```

which fails to compile with an illegal escape character error. OK, so you double up the \ characters to achieve the following:

```
String retval = tmp.replaceAll("d","\\d");
```

This manages to compile, but it returns the bizarre result of no change at all. What's going on here?

Wait—recall that *d*, as a regular expression, doesn't mean a delimited *d* character; it means a digit. Well, of course that wouldn't have worked. Your candidate doesn't have any digits. Try adding another \ character to delimit the *d*:

```
String retval = tmp.replaceAll("d","\\\d");
```

This again fails to compile with an illegal escape character error. This is getting frustrating. Didn't the material in this book say to add a \ character when trying to delimit special characters?

Well, actually, it didn't. The material in this book said to *double* the number of \ characters. Because there are currently two \ characters, doubling them would create *d* as the expression. It looks weird, but try it anyway:

```
String retval = tmp.replaceAll("d","\\\\d");
```

Amazingly, it works! But why did it work? Because the first \ of *d* acts as a delimiter for the second \. Similarly, the third \ acts as a delimiter for the fourth \ character.

OK, that's all clear now. Try to swap out the *$* in *I want to use a $ character* so that the resulting String reads *I want to use a \$ character*. See the FAQs section at the end of this chapter for the solution.

public boolean matches(String regex)

The String.matches method is probably the regex method you'll use most often. It simply compares the given String to a candidate regex and returns true if the two match *exactly* in terms of regular expressions. For example, for the String

```
String num = "4";
```

comparing *4* to *d*, which represents a single digit, will return true:

```
num.matches("\\d");\\returns true
```

However, comparing *4 * (that is, *4* followed by a space) to a digit, *d*, will return false. Similarly, comparing *4* (that is, *4* with no space after it) to *d * (that is, a digit followed by a space) will also return false.

The point here is that, when you use this method, *you have to be careful that the regular expression describes the entirety of the* String *and does not describe anything that is not a part of the* String. Even a space, per the preceding example, can throw your match off-kilter.

Behind the scenes, this method instantiates a Pattern object and simply makes a pass through to the Pattern.matches method discussed earlier. If you're going to be doing a lot of matches operations, you'll probably find it more efficient to explicitly create Pattern and Matcher objects, and use them directly.

If the regular expression passed in is invalid, then this method will throw a PatternSyntaxException error. If the regular expression is null, matches will throw a NullPointerException.

public String replaceFirst (String regex, String replacement)

The String.replaceFirst method replaces the first occurrence of the regex description, with the String represented by the second parameter of this method. Thus, for the String tmp

```
String tmp = "I want to eat 5 hamburgers, 7 days a week";
```

the command

```
String newTmp = tmp.replaceFirst("\d","900");
```

sets newTmp to *I want to eat 900 hamburgers, 7 days a week*.

Behind the scenes, this method instantiates Pattern and Matcher objects, and simply makes a pass through to the Matcher.replaceFirst method discussed earlier. If you're going to be doing a lot of replaceFirst operations, you'll probably find it more efficient to explicitly create Pattern and Matcher objects, and use them directly.

> **NOTE** If you explicitly create `Pattern` and `Matcher` objects and use them directly, you may want to optimize your patterns by putting in end-of-line *$* and beginning-of-line *^* characters where appropriate.

If the regular expression passed in is invalid, then this method will throw a `PatternSyntaxException` error. If the regular expression is null, `replaceFirst` will throw a `NullPointerException`.

public String replaceAll (String regex, String replacement)

The `String.replaceAll` method replaces every occurrence of the regex description with the `String` represented by the second parameter of this method. Thus, for the `String tmp`

```
String tmp = "I want to eat 5 hamburgers, 7 days a week";
```

the command

```
String newTmp = tmp.replaceAll("\d","900");
```

sets `newTmp` to *I want to eat 900 hamburgers, 900 days a week.*

Behind the scenes, this method instantiates `Pattern` and `Matcher` objects, and simply makes a pass through to the `Matcher.replaceAll` method discussed earlier. If you're going to be doing a lot of `replaceAll` operations, you'll probably find it more efficient to explicitly create `Pattern` and `Matcher` objects, and use them directly.

If the regular expression passed in is invalid, then this method will throw a `PatternSyntaxException` error. If the regular expression is null, `replaceFirst` will throw a `NullPointerException`.

public boolean split(String regex)

This method can be particularly helpful if you need to break up a `String` into an array of substrings based on some criteria—in concept, it's similar to the `StringTokenizer`. However, it's much more powerful and more resource intensive than `StringTokenizer` because it allows your program to use a regular expressions as the splitting criteria.

This method always returns at least one element. If the split candidate, input, can't be found, then a String array is returned that contains exactly one String— namely, the original input. If the input can be found, then a String array is returned. That array contains every substring after an occurrence of the input.

Thus, calling the split(",") method on the String *Hello, Dolly*, will return a String array consisting of two elements. The first element of the array will contain *Hello*, and the second will contain *Dolly*.

There are some subtleties you should be aware of when working with this method. If the String had been *Hello,Dolly*, with a trailing comma character after the *y* in *Dolly* then this method would still have returned a two-element String array consisting of *Hello* and *Dolly*. The implicit behavior is that trailing spaces aren't returned.

If the String had been *Hello,,,Dolly*, then the resulting String array would have had four elements. The return value of the split method, as applied to the pattern, is as follows:

```
// "Hello,,,Dolly".split() is equal to {"Hello","","","Dolly"}
```

Behind the scenes, this method instantiates a Pattern object and simply makes a pass through to the Pattern.split method discussed earlier. If you're going to be doing a lot of split operations, you'll probably find it more efficient to explicitly create Pattern objects and use them directly.

If the regular expression passed in is invalid, then this method will throw a PatternSyntaxException error. If the regular expression is null, replaceFirst will throw a NullPointerException.

public String split(String regex, int limit)

This method returns an array containing substrings of the String object it was called on. Those substrings are the text surrounding the regex expression described by the first parameter, regex. The actual number of elements in the array is controlled by the second parameter, limit. The following sections explain what the different values of limit can mean.

Limit == 0

If you specify that the second parameter, limit, should equal 0, then this method returns an array containing as many matching substrings as possible, and trailing spaces are discarded. Thus, the pattern

```
Pattern p = "Hello, Dolly".split(",",0);
```

will return an array consisting of two elements when split against the candidate *Hello, Dolly*.

Similarly, split will return two elements when matched against *Hello, Dolly*, that has a trailing comma after the *y* in *Dolly*:

```
String tmp[] = "Hello, Dolly,.".split(",",0);
```

However, you may not always want this behavior. For example, there may be times when you want to limit the number of elements returned.

Limit > 0

Use a positive limit if you're interested in only a set number of matches. You should use that number plus 1 as the limit. To split *Hello, Dolly, You, Are, My, Favorite* when you want only the first two tokens, you would use this:

```
String[] tmp = "Hello, Dolly, You, Are, My, Favorite".split(",",3);
```

The value of the resulting String is as follows:

```
//tmp[0] is  "Hello"
// tmp[1] is "Dolly";
```

The interesting behavior here is that a third element is returned:

```
//tmp[2] is  "You, Are, My, Favorite";
```

Using a positive limit can potentially lead to performance enhancements, because the regex engine can stop searching when it meets the specified number of matches.

Limit < 0

Using a negative number—any negative number—for the limit tells the regex engine that you want to return as many matches as possible *and* that you want trailing spaces, if any, to be returned. Thus, for the regex pattern , and the candidate *Hello,Dolly*, the command

```
String tmp[] is "Hello,Dolly".split(",", -1);
```

results in

```
//tmp == {"Hello","Dolly"};
```

However, for the String *Hello, Dolly,* which has trailing spaces after the comma following *Dolly*, the method call

```
String tmp[] = "Hello,Dolly,    ".split(",", -1);
```

results in

```
//tmp is equal to {"Hello","Dolly","    "};
```

Notice that the actual value of the negative limit doesn't matter. Thus

```
p.split("Hello,Dolly", -1);
```

is exactly equivalent to

```
p.split("Hello,Dolly", -100);
```

Behind the scenes, this method instantiates a `Pattern` object and simply makes a pass through to the `Pattern.split` method discussed earlier. If you're going to be doing a lot of `split` operations, you'll probably find it more efficient to explicitly create the `Pattern` object and use it directly.

If the regular expression passed in is invalid, then this method will throw a `PatternSyntaxException` error. If the regular expression is null, `replaceFirst` will throw a `NullPointerException`.

Summary

In this chapter, I provided detailed documentation and numerous examples for the `Pattern` and `Matcher` classes and their methods. I also discussed the new regex methods of the `String` class. You should now have a better sense of how some of these objects work and how they work together, and a point of reference when working these methods. In Chapter 3 you'll learn how to integrate these new tools, the regex language, and the Java language proper into a unified whole.

Q: How do I start using the regex package?

A: Simply import the `java.util.regex.*` package.

Q: How do I find out whether a string contains a substring?

A: If you're really looking for a explicit substring, instead of a pattern description, then use the `String.indexOf` method. However, if you need to actually confirm the existence of a pattern, then you have two paths open to you. The first is to use a variation of the `String.split` method with a negative number as the second parameter:

```
String tokens[] = candidate.split(subStringPattern,-1);
```

and make sure the resulting array has more than a single element:

```
boolean isThere = tokens.length > 1? true: false;
```

The problem here is that if the phrase you're looking for just happens to be the last element in the candidate sentence, then size of the array will be still be 1, which will lead to a false conclusion. Try this with the candidate *this is the phrase I want* and the phrase description *want.* with a period trailing the *t* character.

Your second option is to use a short method like the following, which will always work:

```
/**
 * Confirms, or denies, the existence of the regex
 * as part of the candidate String.
 * @param the <code>String</code> candidate
 * @param the <code>String</code> subStringPattern
 * @return <code>boolean</code> true if the regex
 * describes part of the
 * @author M Habibi
 */

public static boolean
containsSubtring(String candidate, String subStringPattern)
{
    boolean retval = false;
    //compile the pattern
    Pattern pattern = Pattern.compile(subStringPattern);
```

```
        //see if any part of the candidate contains the
        //description
        Matcher matcher = pattern.matcher(candidate);
        retval = matcher.find();

        return retval;
    }
```

Q: How do I confirm the existence of the nth occurrence of a substring?

A: The solution here is similar to the one given previously, including the usage of the String.split method. The same limitations apply. As far the method-based solution is concerned, the only modifications that you need to make to the method are the following.

First, adjust the method signature so that it accepts a third parameter as the number of interactions, so that the signature looks like the following:

```
public static boolean containsSubtring(
  String candidate,
  String subStringPattern,
  int n
)
```

Second, add the loop indicated in bold:

```
boolean retval = false;
//compile the patterns
Pattern pattern = Pattern.compile(subStringPattern);

//see if any part of the candidate contains the
//description
Matcher matcher = pattern.matcher(candidate);
for (int i=0; i< n; i++)
{
  retval = matcher.find();
  if (!retval) break;
}
return retval;
```

Q: How do I swap out the $ in I want to use a $ character so that the resulting string reads I want to use a \$ character?

A: For the candidate `String`

```
String candidate = "I want to use a $ character";
```

the solution is the somewhat counterintuitive regex pattern

```
String newString = candidate.replaceAll("\\$","\\\\\\$");
```

The initial parameter, \\$, is clear enough. You want the dollar sign, which just happens to be a regex metacharacter meaning end-of-line. Because you do want the actual dollar sign character and not the end-of-line, you have to delimit the dollar sign, producing the pattern \$.

However, you also need to meet the needs of the `String` object's constructor, which expects to treat anything following a \ as a `String` metacharacter. Because \$ isn't a `String` metacharacter (it's a regex metacharacter), you need to tell the `String` object's constructor to ignore the \. Thus, you need to delimit it once again, producing \\$.

This leads to the second part of the pattern: \\\\\\$. Here, the first \ delimits the second \, the third \ delimits the fourth \, and the fifth \ delimits the sixth. Thus, the `String` \\\\\\$ results in \\\$.

Internally, the method has to rip out the \$ part of *I want to use a $ character* and replace it with *something*, but what is that something? The method has decomposed the original `String` you gave it into two parts: a substring consisting of *I want to use a* and a second substring consisting of *character*.

Normally, the `Matcher.replaceAll` method inserts whatever you give it between these two substrings, concatenates the result, and returns that. However, because what you gave it just happens to contain the dollar symbol, there is an added wrinkle.

As the `Matcher.replaceAll` description in this chapter shows, the dollar sign has special significance in the `replaceAll` method. It's used to refer to a subgroup that has been captured by the pattern. Because you don't want it to have that significance, you need to delimit it again. Hence, the pattern \\\$, in which the first \ delimits the second \, and the third \ delimits the $, thus logically producing \$.

Advanced Regex

"You must turn and face the tiger to learn it is made of paper."
— Zen saying

THIS CHAPTER EXPLORES some of the more advanced features of regular expressions in J2SE. The goal is to provide a point of reference for the more complex regex tools and concepts available to Java developers. This chapter should be a resource you can come back to when you need a refresher on a J2SE regex concept.

Of course, there's no learning tool as useful as actually writing code, so I encourage you to try out these concepts on your own. This chapter introduces a variety of concepts, including groups, subgroups, noncapturing groups, greedy qualifiers, positive qualifiers, reluctant qualifiers, positive lookaheads, negative lookaheads, positive lookbehinds, and negative lookbehinds. The final section of this chapter focuses on increasing the efficiency of your regular expressions.

> **NOTE** The examples in this chapter are intentionally simple so as to clearly illustrate the mechanisms being discussed. More complex examples, such as those used professionally, are explored in Chapter 5 and in the Appendixes.

Understanding Groups

As I explained in Chapter 2, a group is simply a sequence of characters that describes a regex pattern. Thus, $\backslash w \backslash d$ is a group, because there are two characters, $\backslash w$ and $\backslash d$, and they're in a sequence. This is an implicit group and thus trivial, because most groups, as such, are explicitly surrounded by parentheses. In Java regular expressions, every pattern has groups, and they're indexed. Thus, the pattern $\backslash w \backslash d$ has a single group, namely itself, and the index of that group is, of course, 0.

Groups are described in the Pattern but realized in the Matcher. Conceptually, this is similar to how SQL works, where queries are described in the SQL query, but the matching parts are extracted from the ResultSet. Thus, when you describe the pattern $\backslash w \backslash d$, you might extract the matching candidate *A9* from the candidate *A9 is my favorite*. For example, if the group is described as

```
Pattern p = Pattern.compile("\\w\\d");
```

and the candidate String is

```
String candidate = "A9 is my favorite";
```

you define a Matcher for this candidate String:

```
Matcher matcher = p.matcher(candidate);
```

Assuming that the Matcher.find() method has already been called, then calling Matcher.group(0) returns the part of the candidate String that matches the entire pattern, as follows:

```
String tmp = matcher.group(0);
```

Thus, the Matcher.group(0) method is a bit of a misnomer. It doesn't actually extract the group; it extracts the part of the candidate String that matches that group. This is a subtle but important difference. The full example follows in Listing 3-1.

Listing 3-1. Working with Groups

```
import java.util.regex.*;
public class SimpleGroupExample{
    public static void main(String args[]){
        //the original pattern is always group 0
        Pattern p = Pattern.compile("\\w\\d");
        String candidate = "A9 is my favorite";

        //if there is a match, extract that part of
        //the candidate string that matches group(0)
        Matcher matcher = p.matcher(candidate);

        //OUTPUT is 'A9'
        if (matcher.find()){
            String tmp = matcher.group(0);
            System.out.println(tmp);
        }
    }
}
```

That works perfectly when you need the whole pattern. But what about cases in which you need subsections of that pattern? How do you extract those? That's where subgroups come to the rescue.

Understanding Subgroups

Just as a pattern can have groups, so can it have subgroups. *Subgroups* are simply smaller groups within the larger whole. They're separated from the original group, and from each other, by being surrounded by parentheses.

In the example in the preceding section, in order to be able to refer explicitly to the digit *\d*, you modify the pattern to *\w(\d)*. Here, *\w\d* is group(0) and *(\d)* is group(1). Listing 3-2 demonstrates the use of a subgroup to extract the part of the candidate that matches the digit *\d*.

Listing 3-2. Working with Subgroups

```
import java.util.regex.*;
public class SimpleSubGroupExample{
    public static void main(String args[]){
        //the original pattern is always group 0
        Pattern p = Pattern.compile("\\w(\\d)");
        String candidate = "A9 is my favorite";

        //if there is a match, extract the parts that
        //match.
        Matcher matcher = p.matcher(candidate);
        if (matcher.find()){
            //Extract 'A9', which matches group(0), which is
            //always the entire pattern itself.
            String tmp = matcher.group(0);
            System.out.println(tmp); //tmp is 49

            //extract part of the candidate string that matches
            //group(1): Namely, the '9' which follows the 'A'
            tmp = matcher.group(1); //tmp is 9
            System.out.println(tmp);
        }
    }
}
```

Listing 3-2 allows you to extract parts of the candidate String that match the entire expression. It also allows you to extract subsections of that matching section. Thus, you can extract *9* from the matching region *A9* because *9* matches group(1). That is, the regex engine stores the *9* when it matches *A9*, because you defined the subgroup *(\d)*.

Accessing Subgroups

So how does all of this actually work? Are there little fairies running around under the hood of the regex engine, keeping track of all these groups? Well, yes and no.

Although there are no fairies under the hood that I know of, the regex engine is internally tracking all subgroups by putting the matching sections from the candidate String into memory. Thus, because you defined the pattern as *\w(\d)*, the regex will keep track of any single digit when that digit is preceded by an alphanumeric or underscore character. That's what the regex thinks you mean for it do when you put the expression *(\d)* in parentheses.

The engine provides access to these captured groups based on their numeric index. Captured groups are indexed from left to right, in the order of their opening parentheses, and group(0) always refers to the original expression in its entirety. Thus, in the preceding example, group(0) refers to the part of the candidate string that matches the entire expression *\w(\d)*, whereas group(1) refers to the part of the expression that matches the *(\d)* part of the expression.

For example, if your pattern was *(\w)(\d)(\w)(\w)* and your candidate string was *J2SE*, then group 0 would have matched the entire candidate *J2SE*. Group 1 would have matched *J*, group 2 would have matched *2*, group 3 would have matched *S*, and group 4 would have matched *E*.

Correspondingly, if your pattern stayed *(\w)(\d)(\w)(\w)* but your candidate string was *R2D2*, then group 0 would have matched the entire candidate *R2D2*. Group 1 would have matched *R*, group 2 would have matched *2*, group 3 would have matched *D*, and group 4 would have matched *2*.

Noncapturing Subgroups

There may be times when you need to define a group, but you don't want that group to be captured—you simply want to treat it like a single logical entity. The major advantage of using these *noncapturing groups* is that they're less memory intensive because they don't require the regex engine to keep track of the matching parts.

Consider the pattern *(\w)(\d\d)(\w+)*. Specifically, if you don't need access to the trailing *(\w+)*, you can optimize a bit.

To mark a group as noncapturing, you simply follow the opening parameters of that group with the characters *?:*. That is, you can write the expression as *(\w)(\d\d)(?:\w+)*. Notice that the only difference between the original expression, *(\w)(\d\d)(\w+)*, and the new expression, *(\w)(\d\d)(?:\w+)*, is the use of the *?:* that immediately precedes the last group, *(\w+)*.

The most common use of noncapturing groups is for the sake of logical separation. For example, say you need to find out what kind of morning a person is having. You'll accept *good morning, bad morning, terrible morning, great morning*, and so on. For the sake of clarity, you write the expression as *(good|bad|terrible|great) morning*. That is, you want to treat the various kinds of mornings as a single logical unit.

However, say you don't need to capture the type of morning, because you're not going to be using it for anything—you just want to know it's there. You modify your expression to *(?:good|bad|terrible|great) morning*. Specifically, you insert *?:* just inside the group definition, after the opening parenthesis of the group. This gives you the ability to treat the various kinds of mornings as a single logical unit, but it doesn't waste memory capturing the description.

NOTE To make a group noncapturing, insert *?:* inside the opening parenthesis of the group.

An added issue in working with noncapturing groups is that they aren't counted, as far as group indexing is concerned. This makes perfect sense, as you are, in effect, telling the regex engine that you aren't interested in these groups. Thus, why should the regex track them or provide a mechanism that allows you to refer to them? After all, you explicitly told the regex engine that you weren't interested in doing so.

So for the pattern *(?:\w)(\d)*, group(0) is the entire pattern, namely *\w\d*, and group(1) is *(\d)*. Notice that *(?:\w)* is not group(1), as it normally would be, because *(?:\w)* is a noncapturing group; it's preceded by *?:*. Listing 3-3 demonstrates the use of a simple noncapturing subgroup.

Listing 3-3. Working with Noncapturing Subgroups

```java
import java.util.regex.*;

public class NonCapturingGroupExample{
    public static void main(String args[]){
        //define the pattern
        String regex = "hello|hi|greetings|(?:good morning)";

        //define the candidate strings
        String candidate1 = "Tommy say hi to you";
        String candidate2 = "Tommy say good morning to you";
```

```
        //compile the pattern
        Pattern pattern = Pattern.compile(regex);

        //extract the first pattern
        Matcher matcher = pattern.matcher(candidate1);
        //show the number of groups
        System.out.println("GROUP COUNT:"+ matcher.groupCount());

        if (matcher.find())System.out.println("GOT 1:"+candidate1);


        //reuse the matcher, and check the second candidate string
        matcher.reset();
        matcher = pattern.matcher(candidate2);

        //show the number of groups
        System.out.println("GROUP COUNT:"+ matcher.groupCount());

        if (matcher.find())
        System.out.println("GOT 2:" +candidate2);
    }
}
```

The output of this example is shown in Output 3-1.

Output 3-1. Output of NonCapturingGroupExample

```
GROUP COUNT:0
GOT 1:Tommy say hi to you
GROUP COUNT:0
GOT 2:Tommy say good morning to you
```

If you had used a capturing group, then the group count could have been 1. Although this may seem like a fairly innocuous issue, it could grow exponentially more complex, as the number of capturing groups grow.

Back References

Back references are the mechanism you use to access captured subgroups, *while the regex engine is executing*. When I say, *while the regex engine is executing*, you can think of this as the regex engine's runtime. Thus, you can manipulate a subgroup from an earlier part of the match later on in the pattern.

For example, in Chapter 1, I discussed the pattern *\b(\w+) \1\b* to match repeated words. Here, when you use the *\1*, you're asking the regex engine to refer back to it itself and insert whatever had matched the *(\w+)* part of it. Why the *(\w+)* part? Because that is the capturing group with the index of 1. Remember that capturing groups are counted from the rightmost parenthesis, starting with the index of 1.

For a given pattern with subgroups, Java offers three mechanisms for referring to the corresponding group matches. The first, and most object-oriented, mechanism is to use the various `Matcher` object methods. These include the `Matcher.group`, `Matcher.start`, `Matcher.end`, and `Matcher.replaceAll` methods, as discussed in Chapter 2. However, this mechanism doesn't allow the regex pattern to refer back to itself during the regex runtime.

The second approach uses the *\n* nomenclature, where *\n* refers the *n*th capturing group, if it exists. This deserves a bit of explanation. Specifically, what does "if it exists" mean? For an answer, consider the simple regex pattern *(\w)(\d)(\w)* as applied to *W3C*. You could refer to group 0 by using the regex *\0*, group 1 by using *\1*, group 2 by using *\2*, and group 3 by using *\3*. However, *\5* would be meaningless because there's no group *5* in the pattern, as would a reference to *\33*.

Well, yes and no regarding group 33. Although the regex engine knows that there is no group 5, the latter example, group 33, is open to interpretation. That is, the regex engine could, and does, decide that you meant group 3, followed by character *3*. Thus, examining the back reference *\33* from the preceding example would yield *C3*: *C* followed by the character *3*. As shown previously, this mechanism does allow the regex pattern to refer back to itself during runtime.

Finally, there is a third way to refer to back references. Three replacement methods on the `Matcher` object, `appendReplacement`, `ReplaceAll`, and `ReplaceFirst`, as well as the `String` methods `replaceFirst` and `replaceAll`, also allow access to the captured back references by using the *$n* nomenclature, in which *n* represents the index of the group in question. Like the *\n* pattern discussed at the beginning of this section, use of *$n* will prompt the regex engine to take the most liberal interpretation of the pattern possible in order to facilitate a match.

Thus for the pattern *(\w)(\d)(\w)*, using *$33* will prompt the regex engine to assume you meant group 3 followed by the character *3*. This is demonstrated in Listing 3-4.

Listing 3-4. Working with Back References

```java
import java.util.regex.*;

public class ReplaceExample{
    public static void main(String args[]){
        //define the pattern
        String regex = "(\\w)(\\d)(\\w+)";

        //compile the pattern
        Pattern pattern = Pattern.compile(regex);

        //define the candidate string
        String candidate = "X99SuperJava";

        //extract a matcher for the candidate string
        Matcher matcher = pattern.matcher(candidate);

        //return a new string that has replaced
        //every matching part of the candidate string
        //with whatever was found in the third group,
        //followed by the digit three
        String tmp = matcher.replaceAll("$33");
        //returns C3
        System.out.println("REPLACEMENT: " + tmp);
        //notice that the original candidate string
        //is unchanged, as expected. After all, Strings
        //are immutable objects in Java.
        //returns W3C
        System.out.println("ORIGINAL: " + candidate);
    }
}
```

It's important to be careful when you're working with back references. You could be asking the regex engine to do things you had no idea you were asking for, and that, in turn, could cost you in terms of efficiency and/or correctness.

One final word of warning: Calling back references for a group that doesn't exist will cause an IndexOutOfBoundsException to be thrown. Make sure your back references exist before you refer to them.

Greedy Qualifiers

You might have noticed that the third subgroup of the pattern *(\w)(\d\d)(\w+)*, namely *(\w+)*, actually provided the regex engine with some discretion. Given the candidate *X99SuperJava*, the subexpression *(w+)* only had to match one or more word characters to meet its obligation, yet it chose to match them all. That is, it chose to match the candidate *SuperJava* when it could have just matched *S*, *Su*, *Sup*, and so on. After all, these also meet the requirement of being one or more word characters. Why did the engine decide to match as much as possible?

It did so because it is, in a word, *greedy.* The nature of the regex engine is to match as much as it possibly can, so long as that match doesn't interfere with another matching subexpression somewhere else in the pattern. Thus, it matches the entire candidate *SuperJava*. Table 3-1 presents the Java regex greedy qualifiers for your reference.

Table 3-1. Greedy Qualifiers

Regex	Description
?	The preceding is repeated once or not at all.
*	The preceding is repeated zero or more times.
+	The preceding is repeated one or more times.
{n}	The preceding is repeated exactly *n* times.
{n,}	The preceding is repeated at least *n* times.
{n,m}	The preceding is repeated at least *n* times, but no more than *m* times. This includes *m* repetitions.

Greedy matching has an interesting behavioral pattern that I think of as *greedy-generous.* The leftmost part of the pattern, the first *(\w)*, attempts to match as much as possible. When it can't match anymore, the next part of the pattern is evaluated. This is the greedy part.

If that second part of the pattern fails to find any matches, and then the first matching pattern starts to slowly *release characters that it has already collected,* thus providing the second part of the pattern with more opportunities to match. This is the generous part of the behavior.

At this point, one of two things can happen. The first alternative is that the latter group can finally achieve a match, in which case the first group stops releasing characters. The second alternative is that the latter group can fail to match, even with the characters made available to it from the earlier group. If this happens, then the group that was releasing characters, in effect, collects those released characters again, and the regex engine goes on. If a later subexpression again fails to match, then the process is repeated.

So, what does all of this mean to you? Well, quite a bit, really. Consider the regex pattern *(\w+)(\d\d)(\w+)*, which is almost identical to the pattern *(\w)(\d\d)(\w+)* except that first pattern uses + after the first \w, thus forming the group *(\w+)*. That little + can make a huge difference in terms of efficiency, and one that you might not notice in casual use, because the result of applying the new pattern against the candidate *X99SuperJava* doesn't change.

Listing 3-5 examines what actually happens when the pattern is evaluated.

Listing 3-5. Greedy Qualifier Example

```java
import java.util.regex.*;

public class GreedyExample{
    public static void main(String args[]){
        //define the pattern
        String regex = "(\\w+)(\\d\\d)(\\w+)";

        //compile the pattern
        Pattern pattern = Pattern.compile(regex);

        //define the candidate string
        String candidate = "X99SuperJava";

        //extract a matcher for the candidate string
        Matcher matcher = pattern.matcher(candidate);

        matcher.find();

        //extract the matching groups
        System.out.println(matcher.group(1));//returns 'X'
        System.out.println(matcher.group(2));//returns '99'
        System.out.println(matcher.group(3));//returns SuperJava
    }
}
```

When group(1) runs, *(\w+)* examines every character in the candidate String *X99SuperJava*. That is, *X* is explicitly considered, passes inspection, and is put into the matching bag for this group. Because this pattern is greedy and has + after *\w*, it continues. Next, *9* is explicitly considered and passes inspection. Then, the next *9* is considered. This continues until the entire String *X99SuperJava* is consumed.

After group(1) is satisfied, group(2), namely *(\d\d)*, gets an opportunity. Because group(2) is unable to match anything at all, group(1) releases the *a* character at the end of *X99SuperJava*. The *a* character is considered by group(2), found not be a digit, and considered not to be sufficient. Thus, group(1) releases the *v* character. group(2) inspects it, finds it lacking, and rejects it. Thus, group(1) releases the *a* character immediately before the *v* character in *X99SuperJava*. This continues until group(1) has released every character except *X*. Finally, the release of the two *9* characters allow group(2) to match. Now group(1) has *X* and group(2) has *99*.

Finally, group(3) gets an opportunity to run. It starts examining the candidate String *X99SuperJava* at the point immediately following the second *9* character. And because it's greedy, it matches the entire String *SuperJava*.

Thus, the two patterns *(\w)(\d\d)(\w+)* and *(\w+)(\d\d)(\w+)* produce exactly the same result when applied to the String *X99SuperJava* but at vastly different efficiency costs. Although this may be insignificant when you're dealing with a small String, it's very significant when you're parsing a directory full of files; it could mean the difference between your application working and it running out of memory.

Possessive Qualifiers

Given the context of greedy qualifiers, *possessive qualifiers* are relatively easy to understand. They're unique to Java, though they'll probably be adopted by other regex languages in time. Simply put, they're greedy, but never generous. Adding a plus sign (+) after an existing greedy qualifier forms a possessive qualifier. Thus, *\d+* becomes *\d++*, *\d{n,m}* becomes *\d{n,m}+*, and so on.

Consider the previous example in which the pattern *(\w+)(\d\d)(\w+)* is applied to the candidate string *X99SuperJava*. I established earlier that the regex engine, when faced with the group *(\w+)*, would attempt to match as many characters as possible. I also established that it would release those matches if such a release would help a later group achieve a match.

If you don't want the group to release its matches to help later groups match, however, then you would use possessive qualifiers simply by following your last expression with an additional plus sign. You form the pattern *(\w++)(\d\d)(\w+)*— that is, you turn *\w+* into *\w++*.

When the pattern is first run, group(1), namely *(\w++)*, consumes every character in the candidate *X99SuperJava*. However, because of the existence of the second plus sign, the engine refuses to release any of those matching characters to help the following groups match. You find that group(1) matches, and group(2) and group(3) don't—the regex as whole doesn't match. Listing 3-6 demonstrates this.

Listing 3-6. Possessive Qualifier Example

```java
import java.util.regex.*;

public class PossesiveExample{
    public static void main(String args[]){
        //define the pattern
        String regex = "(\\w++)(\\d\\d)(\\w+)";
        //compile the pattern
        Pattern pattern = Pattern.compile(regex);

        //define the candidate string
        String candidate = "X99SuperJava";

        //extract a matcher for the candidate string
        Matcher matcher = pattern.matcher(candidate);

        if (matcher.find()){
            System.out.println("GROUP 0:" +
            matcher.group(0));
            System.out.println("GROUP 1:" +
            matcher.group(1));
            System.out.println("GROUP 2:" + matcher.group(2));
            System.out.println("GROUP 3:" + matcher.group(3));
        }
        else{
            System.out.println("NO MATCHES" );
        }

        System.out.println("Done");
    }
}
```

Reluctant Qualifiers

At the other end of the spectrum from greedy qualifiers are *reluctant qualifiers,* which try to match as little as possible. Reluctant qualifiers are formed by appending *?* to an existing greedy qualifier. Thus, *X+* becomes *X+?, X(n,m}* becomes *X{n,m}?,* and so on. Given the pattern *\d+?* against the candidate string *1234,* for example, the resultant match is *1,* as Listing 3-7 demonstrates.

Listing 3-7. Reluctant Qualifier Example

```java
import java.util.regex.*;

public class ReluctantExample{
    public static void main(String args[]){
        //define the pattern
        String regex = "(\\d+?)";
        //compile the pattern
        Pattern pattern = Pattern.compile(regex);

        //define the candidate string
        String candidate = "1234";

        //extract a matcher for the candidate string
        Matcher matcher = pattern.matcher(candidate);

        while (matcher.find()){
            //matches once for each digit
            //if this were not an example of a
            //reluctant qualifier, it would match
            //exactly once, and that match would
            //include every digit in the candidate
            //string "1234".
            System.out.println(matcher.group());

        }

        System.out.println("Done");
    }
}
```

Every time find() is run, it matches as little as possible, because it's *reluctant* to match. The Pattern matches exactly four times: once for each digit. If you weren't using a reluctant qualifier in the Pattern, there would have been a single match for the entire candidate string, namely *1234*, because the Pattern would have been greedy and matched as much as possible.

Understanding Lookarounds

There are times in programming, as in life, when you'd like to know what to expect before making a more serious effort. For example, you might want to know that your favorite restaurant is open before you go there to eat. How would you accomplish that? You would, of course, phone ahead. The same idea is used in regex lookarounds.

There are four flavors of lookarounds: positive lookaheads, negative lookaheads, positive lookbehinds, and negative lookbehinds. The following sections explain each in detail.

> **NOTE** Lookarounds are noncapturing groups, but they never consume text. Thus, verifying that a certain character exists further down the candidate string doesn't mean that the character in question has been exhausted by the regex pattern. Lookaheads don't match characters; they match positions.

Positive Lookaheads

Positive lookaheads allow your regex to "peek ahead" and make sure that the pattern does, in fact, exist somewhere down the line in your candidate string before the rest of the match is attempted. They don't consume that text, however—they just confirm the truth of its existence. They are, basically, a way to tell the regex engine "Don't bother looking at the candidate string if it doesn't have the lookahead." You form them by opening the group with the characters *(?=*. For example, the lookahead

```
(?=\d\d)
```

confirms that the candidate string contains two digits in a row. However, it doesn't consume those two digits. Combined with other regex patterns, positive lookaheads can a very powerful weapon in your regex arsenal.

Say you want to match IP addresses, but only if they begin with *255*. Also, if they do begin with *255*, you want the entire regex pattern. With lookaheads, this issue is easily solved, as demonstrated in Listing 3-8. Of course, this example assumes a great deal about the friendly nature of the data. Even so, it does nicely illustrate the usage of lookaheads, so all is forgiven. Table 3-2, which follows Listing 3-8, deconstructs the regex pattern *(?=^255).**.

Listing 3-8. Simple Positive Lookahead Example

```java
import java.util.regex.*;

public class PositiveLookaheadExample{
    public static void main(String args[]){
        //define the pattern
        String regex = "(?=^255).*";

        //compile the pattern
        Pattern pattern = Pattern.compile(regex);

        //define the candidate string
        String candidate = "255.0.0.1";

        //extract a matcher for the candidate string
        Matcher matcher = pattern.matcher(candidate);

        String ip ="not found";

        //if the candidate starts with 255, then the ip
        //will be populated with the correct information.
        if (matcher.find())
            ip=matcher.group();

        String msg ="ip: " + ip;

        System.out.println(msg);
    }
}
```

Table 3-2. The Pattern (?=^255).*

Regex	Description
(?=	A positive lookahead consisting of
^	The beginning of line character followed by
2	The character 2 followed by
5	The character 5 followed by
5	The character 5 followed by
)	Close the lookahead group
.	Any character
*	Repeated zero or more times

* **In English:** Capture the entire IP address if it starts with 255.

In Listing 3-8, the regex engine first confirms that the candidate string starts with *255* before attempting to execute the rest of the pattern. If the candidate String doesn't do so, then the rest of the pattern can't possibly match and no resources are wasted in attempting to do so.

Notice that using a noncapturing group *(?:=^255)* instead of *(?=^255)* to confirm the existence of *255* wouldn't work, because *(?:=^255)* consumes the characters *255*, even though it doesn't capture them, and returns the *.0.0.1* that follows them.

Negative Lookaheads

Negative lookaheads, like positive lookaheads, allow your regex to "peek ahead." However, they allow the engine to confirm that something does *not* exist somewhere down the line in your candidate string. Like all lookaheads, they don't consume text; they just confirm the truth of its absence. They're formed by opening the group with the characters *(?!.* For example:

```
(?!\d\d)
```

confirms that the candidate String doesn't contain two digits in a row. It doesn't consume those two digits.

Say you're parsing text and you want find reference to *John* and extract both the first name and the last name, unless that reference happens to *John Smith*. With negative lookaheads, this sort of exercise becomes very easy. Listing 3-9 demonstrates the code for doing so. Table 3-3 deconstructs the regex pattern used.

Listing 3-9. Simple Negative Lookahead Example

```java
import java.util.regex.*;
public class NegativeLookaheadExample{
    public static void main(String args[])
    throws Exception
    {
        //define the pattern
        String regex = "John (?!Smith)[A-Z]\\w+";

        //compile the pattern
        Pattern pattern = Pattern.compile(regex);

        String candidate = "I think that John Smith ";
        candidate +="is a fictional character. His real name ";
        candidate +="might be John Jackson, John Westling, ";
        candidate +="or John Holmes for all we know.";

        //extract a matcher for the candidate string
        Matcher matcher = pattern.matcher(candidate);

        String tmp=null;

        //extract the matching group. Notice that it's
        //the default group, since lookarounds are
        //noncapturing
        while (matcher.find()){
            tmp=matcher.group();
            System.out.println("MATCH:" + tmp);
        }
    }
}
```

*Table 3-3. The Pattern **John (?!Smith)[A-Z]\\w+***

Regex	Description
J	The character *J* followed by
o	The character *o* followed by
h	The character *h* followed by
n	The character *n* followed by
<space>	A space, followed by
(?!	A position in which you'll find anything but
S	The character *S* followed by
m	The character *m* followed by
i	The character *i* followed by
t	The character *t* followed by
h	The character *h* followed by
)	Close the lookahead group, followed by
[A-Z]	Any uppercase character followed by
\w	A word character
+	Repeated one or more times followed by
\w	Any word character
*	Repeated zero or more times

* **In English:** Find and capture occurrences of *John* followed by some capitalized word, unless that word is *Smith*.

In Listing 3-9, the regex engine first parses the candidate and considers successful matches to be those that consist of *John* when it's followed by some capitalized word, unless that capitalized word is *Smith*. Again, it's important to notice that using a noncapturing group allows you to capture the entire match, because it hasn't been consumed.

Positive Lookbehinds

So far, you've explored the ability to look to the right of the candidate String to "peek ahead" and see what the future has in store for your pattern. Similarly, there are times when it's useful to be able to look to the left of the current position being considered to see what the past had to say about a particular pattern. That is the purpose of *lookbehinds*.

Like lookaheads, lookbehinds come in two flavors. *Positive lookbehinds* confirm the existence of a pattern to the left of the current position, and *negative lookbehinds* confirm the *absence* of a pattern to the left of the current pattern. You form positive lookbehinds by opening a noncapturing group with *(?<=*. Thus, to confirm that two digits preceded the current expression, you might use the following positive lookbehind:

```
(?<=\d\d).*
```

This confirms that the candidate string was preceded by two digits in a row. It doesn't consume those two digits; however, it acts like it did because *they're beyond the scope of the capture*. This happens because the expression parser has already moved past them. That is, the parse has, by definition, already tried to match them and failed to do so. It if hadn't, it would have stopped trying to find the next match.

Consider the candidate *42 is the answer*. When the regex engine compares this candidate `String` against the pattern *(?<=\d\d).**, it starts by examining the first character, which is *4*. Because two digits don't precede *4*, it's rejected. Next, the engine compares the *2* character. Because *2* is also not preceded by two digits, it is discarded. Next, the regex engine examines the space character following *2* in the candidate string *42 is the answer*. Because that space character is, in fact, preceded by two digits, namely *4* and *2*, the regex engine happily starts to match. Of course, because the remaining part of the pattern is *.**, every remaining character is matched. Thus, the space following *42* and everything thereafter is captured. But *4* and *2* aren't captured, because the regex engine already passed them.

Because the regex engine is already past the *4* and the *2* characters, it won't match them. This is an important and subtle distinction. Lookbehinds, like all lookarounds, are noncapturing. However, in this case, they appear to act as if they've already captured the *4* and the *2* characters. That is, the characters *4* and *2* are excluded from the capture set. However, that's because they've already been parsed, not because they've been captured. It's important to be able to see through this illusion.

Listing 3-10 demonstrates some code for using positive lookbehinds. The goal is to parse a document's content and extract any URLs used. Table 3-4 deconstructs the regex pattern used.

Listing 3-10. Simple Positive Lookbehind Example

```java
import java.util.regex.*;
public class PositiveLookBehindExample{
    public static void main(String args[])
    throws Exception
    {

        //define the pattern
        String regex = "(?<=http://)\\S+";

        //compile the pattern
        Pattern pattern = Pattern.compile(regex);

        String candidate = "The Apress website can be found at ";
        candidate +="http://www.apress.com. There, ";
        candidate +="you can find information about some of ";
        candidate +="best books in the industry, including the ";
        candidate +=" bestselling Sun Certified Java Developer ";
        candidate +=" Exam with J2SE(";
        candidate +="http://www.apress.com/book/bookDisplay.";
        candidate +="html?bID=39) as well as others.";



        //extract a matcher for the candidate string
        Matcher matcher = pattern.matcher(candidate);

        //if the url was found, print it out here.
        while (matcher.find()){
            String msg =":"+ matcher.group()+":";
            System.out.println(msg);
        }
    }
}
```

*Table 3-4. The Pattern (?<=**http://**)\S+*

Regex	Description
(?<=	Open a positive lookbehind group consisting of
h	The character *h* followed by
t	The character *t* followed by
t	The character *t* followed by
p	The character *p* followed by
:	The character *:* followed by
/	The character / followed by
/	The character / followed by
\S	A nonspace character
+	Repeated one or more times

* **In English:** Match a URL if that URL is preceded by *http://*.

Negative Lookbehinds

Negative lookbehinds confirm the *absence* of a pattern to the left of the current pattern. They're a way of telling the regex engine, "I'm interested in the candidate String, so long as it isn't preceded by such and such." You form negative lookbehinds by opening a noncapturing group with *(?<!*.

Negative lookbehinds aren't as intuitive as the other lookarounds, so it's worthwhile to explore how they actually work. For example, consider the following negative lookbehind:

```
(?<!\d\d).*
```

The preceding seems to request that the candidate string not be preceded by two digits in a row. However, when you actually test it against the String *42 is the answer*, it matches the entire candidate. What's going on here?

The problem is that the first element in the candidate *42 is the answer* is *4*. So the engine asks itself if the *4* character is preceded by two digits. Because the answer is no, the entire pattern is matched into group(0). Remember, .* is a greedy qualifier, so it matches as much as possible—in this case, the entire candidate string.

Zen and the Art of Efficient Expressions

This section deals presents some techniques you can use to optimize your regular expressions in J2SE. It's designed to help you deal with regular expressions that already exist, as well as establish a framework for writing new ones. The suggestions in this section, along with your own intuition and an active awareness of the nature of your data, will help you optimize your own regex.

Use Noncapturing Groups Where Possible

Capturing groups requires that the JVM keep track of them. This can be very helpful if you need to extract the groups or if you need back references to them later on in the expression. However, if you're using groups strictly for logical purposes, it's worthwhile to make them noncapturing, as this conserves memory use.

The example given earlier for the pattern *(?:good|bad|terrible|great) morning* groups the various kinds of mornings into a logical unit, but it has no need to capture them. Thus, the group is noncapturing and opens with *?:* inside the opening parenthesis.

Precheck Your Candidate Strings

If you're looking for a specific string, you might save CPU cycles by first making sure that the string in question actually exists in your candidate. For example, say you want to parse a string that might contain an e-mail address, and if it does, you want to extract the domain of the e-mail address. It makes sense to first make sure that the candidate contains an @ symbol, and then begin the regex search. Thus, the following is an inexpensive way to check for the necessity of even compiling your pattern:

```
if (candidate.indexOf("@")) //..try to extract domain information.
```

Offer the Most Likely Alternative First

Say your regular expression is designed to validate the title of members of an all-physicians' health club. You expect 90 percent of your clients to have the title *Dr*, but some might not. Thus, you title-matching pattern should probably be something along the lines of *.*\b(?:Dr|Mr|Mrs|Miss|Brother|Mister) .*.

This pattern increases the likelihood of a successful match happening sooner rather than later, thus reducing the number of processes the regex engine has to step through. For example, imagine that the candidate string is *Please meet Dr Hana Saez.* The way the pattern is currently written, the engine will match the *D*, the *r*, the space, and everything thereafter on the first pass. Thus, it will never attempt *Mr*, *Mrs*, and so on.

However, if the pattern had been *.*\b(?:Mr|Mrs|Miss|Brother|Mister| Dr) .**, the engine would have stepped through the entire candidate string once for *Mr*, then again for *Mrs*, then again for *Miss*, then again for *Brother*, and so on until it finally matched *Dr*. The actual result would been the same, but the net path there would have been much more resource intensive.

Be As Specific As Possible

If you know that your regex pattern should only match numbers at a given point, then don't use *\w* to define that part of the match—use *\d*. This will allow the regex engine to narrow the scope of its search and filter more quickly. Or, if you know that your pattern must contain a given word, then use that very word in the pattern. This is the same principle that makes it easier for you to write code to specific requirements. The more focused and detailed the requirements, the easier your job becomes.

For example, say you know that your candidate string must start with a capital letter, with lowercase letters following the initial character. It's more efficient to use a pattern such as *[A-Z][a-z]+* than it is use a pattern such as *\w**. Both might work, but *[A-Z][a-z]+* allows the engine to produce an accurate result faster than *\w**, because it can refuse to consider digits and lowercase letters for the first character, and refuse to consider digits and uppercase letters for the latter parts.

The J2SE regex implementation is much faster with literal strings than it is with characters classes—it can literally zero-in on specific strings. Thus, if you're looking for a number between 10 and 19, it's more efficient to use *1\d* than to use *\d+*, *\d\d*, *\d{2}*, or any such variation.

Specify the Position of Your Match

If you know that the candidate string can only occur after a beginning of line, or right before an end of line, or after punctuation, then say so in your regex. The pattern *^Beth* will match faster and more efficiently than the pattern *Beth*, when you know that it must occur after a newline.

This type of optimization can be particularly powerful because it allows the engine to stop searching after examining only the first two characters of the candidate string. Look for opportunities to take advantage of this sort of thing in your regex.

Specify the Size of Your Match

If you're looking for a match that must be at least *n* characters long, then say so in your regex. Or, if you know that your match can't be more then *m* characters long, say that too.

For example, imagine that you're parsing a large file for references to first names. It's probably reasonable to assume that the names you want contain fewer than 20 characters. So, although you could use a pattern like *\b[A-Z][a-z]+*, it's probably better to use something like *\b[A-Z][a-z]{1,20}*, because the engine can abandon any searches that are longer than 20 characters. Or, if you know that your candidate string must be six or more characters, it's better to use *\w\w\w\w\w\w+* than *\w+*.

> **NOTE** J2SE regex finds specific repetitions much more quickly than quantified ones. Thus, *\w\w\w\w\w\w* is much faster than *\w{6}*.

Limit the Scope of Your Alternatives

It's generally more efficient to offer small alternatives than to offer large ones, and it's better to offer them later than earlier. Thus, if you have the pattern *Good Morning|Good Evening*, you would be better served by the pattern *Good (?:Morning|Evening)*. In the latter example, the regex engine doesn't have to make any decisions until after it has established that *Good* is part of the candidate string.

In the former example, the engine might be obligated to look twice, even if the candidate string doesn't contain the word *Good*. That is, even if the candidate string is *Bad year* and can't possibly match, the pattern **Good Morning|Good Evening** searches twice anyway: once for *Good morning* and then again for *Good Evening*.

Summary

This chapter provided explanations, details, and examples of some of the more challenging tools and concepts in the J2SE regex package. The chapter discussed groups, subgroups, noncapturing groups, greedy qualifiers, positive qualifiers, reluctant qualifiers, positive lookaheads, negative lookaheads, positive lookbehinds, and negative lookbehinds. Finally, the chapter finished with a few tips for optimizing your expressions. The next chapter will introduce some suggestions for working with regular expressions in an object-oriented language such as Java.

FAQs

Q: How do I make a group noncapturing?

A: To make a group noncapturing, insert *?:* inside the opening parenthesis of the group. For example, change *(\w)* to *(?:\w)*.

Q: Given the expression \w(\d(\w)), what's the capturing index of the rightmost subgroup, (\w)?

A: Groups are counted from left to right, starting with the opening parenthesis, and group(0) always refers to the whole regex pattern. Thus, the capturing index of subgroup *(\w)* is 2. Accordingly, the capturing index of *(\d(\w))* is group(2).

Q: How is group indexing affected when one of the groups is a noncapturing group?

A: The noncapturing group isn't counted in any way when group indexes are calculated.

CHAPTER 4

Object-Oriented Regex

"Creativity is allowing yourself to make mistakes.
Art is knowing which ones to keep."
— Scott Adams

IN THIS CHAPTER, I provide some suggestions for using regular expressions in the context of a fully object-oriented language such as Java. This can, and often should, be a different experience than in more procedural languages, because Java offers a different toolset. This chapter covers when to use the `java.util.regex` package, when not to use it, and when to complement the `java.util.regex` package with other Java features.

Regular expressions, as formulated in Java, have a lot in common with the principles that guide Java Database Connectivity (JDBC). JDBC uses a generic descriptive language, Structured Query Language (SQL), for describing and manipulating information, whereas the `java.util.regex` package uses regular expressions. SQL provides a general `Command` object to "compile" that description, just as regex uses the `Pattern` object. SQL provides a `ResultSet` to return the results of that search, whereas regex uses a `Matcher`. The general pattern of use in both JDBC and the regex package is similar. Namely, both provide a generic description, compile it in one object, and examine the results in another object.

It only makes sense to take advantage of the relevant lessons from JDBC programming when you work with regex in Java. The combination of JDBC and general Java principles that I've found to be useful are as follows:

- Optimize your connections.

- Batch reads and writes.

- Store your patterns externally.

- Compile your `Pattern` as you need to.

- Don't limit yourself to a regex solution.

Optimize Your Connections

When you work with regular expressions, use FileChannels over other means of accessing a file. That is, instead of using a RandomAccessFile, a FileInputStream, or a FileOutputStream, gain access to your file using a FileChannel.

Although a detailed discussion of FileChannels is beyond the scope of this book, I do want to briefly touch upon them. FileChannels are Java's latest effort at high-performance file input/output (I/O), and they seem to be very successful. Under the covers, they're optimized for whatever operating system you happen to be on, so they're at least as fast and efficient as their java.io.* counterparts—as a matter of fact, they're often much faster. They also offer tools such as FileLocks, the ability to position anywhere in the file, the ability to read and write concurrently, and the ability to map directly to memory buffers.

> **NOTE** FileChannels also interact better with Threads, but that's a completely different topic that's beyond the scope of this discussion.

FileChannels work by reading data at the byte level and storing it into a ByteBuffer. Thus, the code to read the contents of a file by using a FileChannel might look like Listing 4-1. To learn more about ByteBuffers and Channels in general, please consult Sun's documentation.

Listing 4-1. Using FileChannels to Access a File

```java
import java.io.*;
import java.nio.*;
import java.nio.channels.*;

/**
 * Provides an easy mechanism for extracting the regex contents
 * of a file
 */
public class FileChannelExample{
    public static void main(String args[]) throws IOException{
        //open a connection to the source code for this
        //class
        FileInputStream fis =
        new FileInputStream("FileChannelExample.java");
```

```
        //get a file channel
        FileChannel fc = fis.getChannel();

        //create a ByteBuffer that is large enough
        //and read the contents of the file into it
        ByteBuffer bb = ByteBuffer.allocate((int)fc.size());

        fc.read(bb);
        bb.flip();

        //save the content of the file as a String
        String  fileContent= new String(bb.array());

        //release the FileChannel
        fc.close();
        fc = null;

        //write out the contents of this file
        System.out.println("fileContent = " + fileContent);

    }
}
```

The process is very simple and offers a great many advantages over conventional file access. Basically, you open obtain a FileChannel, read its content into a ByteBuffer or one of its child classes, and then examine that buffer. This is fairly easy to follow in Listing 4-1, because the relevant sections of the code appear in bold. As you can see, if you need to, you can easily convert that data into a String. The advantages you're most concerned with here, of course, relate to speed and memory usage, but there are lot of other, nonregex reasons to use FileChannels.

Batch Reads and Writes

Another important connection issue is the willingness to read the entire contents of a file into memory while you work. Although this principle can sometimes backfire with extremely large files, I've found that it generally works out well for me. The most expensive part of your operations is often going to be the I/O transaction time. It may be imminently reasonable to trade memory for I/O usage, and thus save repeated I/O calls, depending on your situation.

Generally speaking, I've found that I'm better off reading the content into memory, manipulating it there, and then writing it back to the file as I need to.

I've found this more efficient than reading a bit of a file, making some changes, writing those out, reading more of the file, and so on.

> **NOTE** If I'm working with very large files, I've sometimes found it necessary to ignore the preceding advice and actually read parts of the data at a time. That's because a pattern can easily describe a section that might require a match at the beginning of the file as well as the end, thus potentially requiring you to keep the entire file in memory. With extremely large files, this is simply not possible.
>
> In these sorts of scenarios, I'll optimize my expressions to the best of my ability and apply them a section at a time. If that's not sufficient, I'll write a custom Java program that's uniquely designed to parse the specific file. The first pass might look for the opening sequence, the second pass might look within that section for a submatch, and so on.

Store Your Patterns Externally

Storing your regex pattern description in an external file offers three important advantages. The first is that the Pattern doesn't have to be delimited once again for the String constructor, so it's easier to read. The second is a direct corollary of the first, in that the first makes it easier to use generic, non-Java-delimited regular expressions in your code. The third is that extracting the actual pattern to an external file allows you to change the pattern later without having to recompile the class.

> **NOTE** In this context, when I use the term "Java-delimited," I mean the double delimiting of the \ character with the \\ character in Strings.

A Java regex pattern can be a little confusing, especially to someone unfamiliar with how the String and regex delimiters work together. For example, consider the following e-mail descriptor, which is freely available from http://www.regexlib.com. It's difficult enough to parse out exactly what *^([a-zA-Z0-9_\-\.]+)@((\[[0-9]{1,3}\.[0-9]{1,3}\.[0-9]{1,3}\.)|(([a-zA-Z0-9\-]+\.)+))([a-zA-Z]{2,4}|[0-9]{1,3})(\]?)$* means without having to add the somewhat awkward \\ characters that the String object's constructor requires. It's enough to make you reconsider using regex altogether.

Also, the process of changing the regex to be Java-delimited strings introduces fat-finger risks. Unsurprisingly, because your Java regex won't look conventional, it's that much more difficult to solicit help from regex gurus, most of whom are probably more familiar with Perl.

It's also very possible that as your requirements evolve, you may need to change the regular expression without changing any other part of the code. Thus, it's a good idea to store your regex patterns in an external file and then retrieve them when you need them. This offers an opportunity to kill two birds with one stone, because you would, conceivably, store your regex patterns externally and in such a manner that the double delimiting isn't required. But which persistence mechanism should you use? The next few sections discuss some options.

Don't Use Normal Property Files to Store Patterns

At first glance, the solution to storing patterns externally seems to be property files. They're already in place, tried and true, easy to use, easy to modify, intuitive in format, and object oriented. However, Java property files are, unfortunately, not quite up to the task, because of three very strong objections.

The first objection is that property values need to be delimited exactly as Strings need to be delimited in order to work properly. That is, the pattern *\w* would have to be stored as *\\w*, and the pattern *^([a-zA-Z0-9_\-\.]+)@((\ [[0-9]{1,3}\.[0-9]{1,3}\.[0-9]{1,3}\.)|(([a-zA-Z0-9\-]+\.)+))([a-zA-Z]{2,4}| [0-9]{1,3})(\]?)$* becomes the unwieldy

```
^([a-zA-Z0-9_\\-\\.]+)@((\\[[0-9]{1,3}\\.[0-9]{1,3}\\.[0-
9]{1,3}\\.)|(([a-zA-Z0-9\\-]+\\.)+))([a-zA-Z]{2,4}|[0-
9]{1,3})(\\]?)$
```

This is hardly an improvement as far as legibility is concerned.

Second, Properties objects preprocess certain characters, including *\t*, *\n*, and \\. That is, you have to understand the internal mechanisms of how the Properties object stores "special" characters before you use them to store your regex pattern. This is hardly an improvement, as far as abstraction is concerned.

Finally, property files internally use the \ character to delimit the end of a line, so that it can be continued on the next line. Thus, the property file entry

```
Produce = carrots, \
lettuce
```

is read as

```
Produce = carrots, lettuce
```

Accordingly, using `Properties` objects actually increases the complexity of the pattern, because it introduces new things you have to know about in addition to the regex. Again, this is hardly an improvement as far as ease of maintenance is concerned. All things considered, using property files to store regex patterns seems like an invitation for bugs. We can do better.

Don't Use XML to Store Patterns

XML is also a reasonable candidate for external storage of regex patterns. On the positive side, XML is an easy, universally accepted way to keep external system data, and there are many ways to access that data. As a matter of fact, J2SE 1.4 offers the extraordinarily useful `XMLEncoder` and `XMLDecoder` classes, which make it easier than ever to persist and retrieve XML data. `XMLEncoder` and `XMLDecoder` are new Java classes that can help store JavaBeans as serialized XML—better yet, the XML is human readable and maintainable, so changing the XML actually changes the attributes of the object when it is deserialized. Moreover, depending on which XML persistence mechanism you use, the XML parsers may not require you to Java-delimit your patterns.

There are two big problems with the XML persistence approach, however. The first problem is that the easiest XML persistence mechanism, the `XMLEncoder` and `XMLDecoder` classes, decorate `Strings` as they're stored. Thus, the < character becomes *&lt*, > becomes *&gt*, and so on. Second, the XML persistence mechanism, simply by virtue of being XML, has a lot of cluttering metadata that isn't germane to regex. But the proof, as they say, is in the pudding. To illustrate this point, let's try an XML-based approach in the next section and see how it works out.

XML Persistence Example

Because you want to try storing your regular expressions as XML, you'll create a regex-friendly `JavaBean`, say `Regex.java`, that has two member variables: a `String` to hold the regex itself and a `String` description to explain what it's supposed to do. Listing 4-2 lists the code for the `Regex` bean. The idea is to easily store the `Regex` bean as XML by using `XMLEncoder`, thus making modifications to the XML easier.

Listing 4-2. The Regex Bean

```
/**
* Holds a regex-friendly object, so that we can try
* persisting regex descriptions as XML
*/
```

```java
public class Regex implements  java.io.Serializable {

    /**
    * sets the String description
    *
    *@param String description
    */
    public void setDescription(String description){
        this.description = description;
    }

    /**
    * gets String description
    *
    *@return String description
    */
    public String getDescription(){
        return this.description;
    }

    /**
    * sets the String regex
    *
    *@param String regex
    */
    public void setRegex(String regex){
        this.regex = regex;
    }

    /**
    * gets String regex
    *
    *@return String regex
    */
    public String getRegex(){
        return this.regex;
    }

    private String regex;
    private String description;
}
```

Next, you write the persistence code. I'm not going to delve into how to use the XMLEncoder and XMLDecoder objects; that is both off-topic and very easy to figure out from reading Listing 4-3. For a reference on XMLEncoder and XMLDecoder, please review Sun's documentation.

The regex pattern you're storing in this case, *<((?i)TITLE>)(.*?)</\1*, extracts the content of the first title element from an HTML file. See the "FAQs" section for a precise breakdown of how this works.

Listing 4-3. The Persistence Code

```java
import java.io.*;
import java.beans.*;

/**
* Helps persist a Serializable object to XML
* and back again.
*/
public class XMLHelper{
    public static void main(String args[]){
        Regex regex = new Regex();
        regex.setRegex("<((?i)TITLE>)(.*?)</\\1");

        String desc =
        "extracts the title element from an html page";

        regex.setDescription(desc);

        saveXML(regex, "htmlTitle.xml");

    }

    /**
    * Saves the Serializable as an XML file
    * @param ser the object to persist
    * @param fileName the file to save it to.
    */
    public static void saveXML(Serializable ser, String fileName){
```

```
    try{
        XMLEncoder e = new XMLEncoder(
        new BufferedOutputStream(
        new FileOutputStream(fileName)));
        e.writeObject(ser);
        e.close();
    }
    catch(IOException ioe){
        ioe.printStackTrace();
    }

}
/**
* get the Serializable from XML file
* @param fileName the file to get the data from.
* @return ser the object to persist
*/
public static Serializable getXML(String fileName){
Serializable retval= null;
try{
    XMLDecoder d = new XMLDecoder(
    new BufferedInputStream(
    new FileInputStream(fileName)));
    retval = (Serializable)d.readObject();
    d.close();

}
catch(IOException ioe){
    ioe.printStackTrace();
}

return retval;

}
}
```

The XMLHelper class has two methods, saveXML and getXML, which persist and retrieve the state of the object. The XML for the Regex object stored appears in Listing 4-4.

Listing 4-4. The XML State of the Persisted Regex Object

```
<?xml version="1.0" encoding="UTF-8"?>
<java version="1.4.1" class="java.beans.XMLDecoder">
 <object class="Regex">
  <void property="description">
   <string>extracts the title element from an html page</string>
  </void>
  <void property="regex">
    <string>&lt;((?i)TITLE&gt;)(.*?)&lt;/\1</string>
  </void>
 </object>
</java>
```

As you can see, most of this information is human legible and easy to maintain. If you were to change this XML file and deserialize the object, the deserialized object would reflect your changes. That's pretty powerful, but still not as robust as we would like. You'll notice the line

```
<string>&lt;((?i)TITLE&gt;)(.*?)&lt;/\1</string>
```

actually changed the input, as predicted, from using the < character to using *&lt* and the > character to using *&gt*. That's not particularly conducive to readability. Also, you'll notice that the XML has a great deal of metadata about the type of the object, the name of the method, and so on. We don't need any of this. All in all, this is an improvement over the Properties approach, but we can do better still.

> **NOTE** Observant readers may have noticed that manually changing the XML element to be a CDATA section can change the issue of XML decoration and still allow the object deserialization process to work. However, as far as I know, that behavior isn't guaranteed to be platform independent, and it still doesn't address the metadata clutter issue.

Use FileChannels and ByteBuffers to Store Patterns

The Java new I/O (NIO) paradigm offers an easy and elegant solution for externalizing patterns. Without digging too deeply into NIO, you can use the code in Listing 4-5 to extract a regex pattern from a persisted file.

Listing 4-5. Extract a Non-Java-Delimited Regex Pattern from a File

```java
import java.util.regex.*;
import java.io.*;
import java.nio.*;
import java.nio.channels.*;

/**
* Provides an easy mechanism for extracting the regex contents
* of a file
*/
public class RegexHelper{

   /**
    * Extracts the contents of the given file. This
    * particular extraction process is specifically
    * expecting the content of the file to be a
    * non-Java-delimited regex pattern.
    *
    * @param fileName the name of the file that
    * has the regex pattern.
    * @returns a string holding the content of the file
    * @author Mehran Habibi
    **/
   public static String getRegex(String fileName){
    String retval = null;
    try
    {
        //open a connection to the file
        FileInputStream fis =
        new FileInputStream(fileName);

        //get a file channel
        FileChannel fc = fis.getChannel();

        //create a ByteBuffer that is large enough
        //and read the contents of the file into it
        ByteBuffer bb = ByteBuffer.allocate((int)fc.size());

        fc.read(bb);
        bb.flip();
```

```
        //persist the content of the file as a String
        retval = new String(bb.array());

        //release the FileChannel
        fc.close();
        fc = null;

    }
    catch(IOException ioe)
    {
        ioe.printStackTrace();
    }

    return retval;
    }
}
```

Of course, it's not necessary to use `FileChannel`s here; any mechanism that performs a byte-level read of a file would have yielded the same result. However, because reading bytes is so natural with NIO, it seems like the best overall solution. The result here is that a file could contain nothing but a pure regex pattern, without the Java delimitation, and still continue to work properly.

> **NOTE** Make sure that the pattern doesn't have any extra spaces or returns after the last character, as that will be read in as part of the pattern proper and cause your searches to fail.

Of course, this isn't as friendly as it could be—it would be nice, for example, if you could treat the file like a property file and define various keys in it. After all, you don't want to be forced to have a separate file for each regex pattern. For example, you could pass in a key, along with the filename, so that you could store numerous patterns in the same file. With this in mind, add the overloaded method `getRegex`, as shown in Listing 4-6.

Listing 4-6. Overloaded getRegex Method

```
/**
 * Extracts the contents of the given file at the given key.
 * This particular extraction process is specifically
 * expecting the content of the file to be a
 * non-Java-delimited regex pattern.
 *
 * @param fileName the name of the file that
 * has the regex pattern.
 * @param key the key that defines the regex in the file
 * @returns a string holding the content of the file
 * @author Mehran Habibi
 **/
public static String getRegex(String fileName, String key){
 String retval = null;

 //get content of the file
 String content = getRegex(fileName);

 //if the file has content, then try to find the key
 if (content != null)
 {
  //look for a beginning of line, followed by the key,
  //followed by an equal sign, and capture everything between
  //that key and the end of the line.
  String keyRegex = "^"+key+"=(.*)$";

  //we expect the output to have multiple lines
  Pattern pattern = Pattern.compile(keyRegex,Pattern.MULTILINE);

  //extract the matcher, and look for the value to the key
  Matcher matcher = pattern.matcher(content);

  if (matcher != null && matcher.find())
     retval = matcher.group(1);

 }

 return retval;
 }
```

The point here is that you can use and write your regex patterns in a non-Java-specific syntax, at least as far as the double delimiting of the String syntax is concerned. Try testing this code with the sample data shown in Listing 4-7.

Listing 4-7. Sample Content of a Regex Cache File

```
#Email validator that adheres directly to the specification
#for email address naming. It allows for everything from
#ipaddress and country-code domains to very rare characters
#in the username.
email=^([a-zA-Z0-9_\-\.]+)@((\[[0-9]{1,3}\.[0-9]{1,3}\.[0-
9]{1,3}\.)|(([a-zA-Z0-9\-]+\.)+))([a-zA-Z]{2,4}|[0-
9]{1,3})(\]?)$

#Matches UK postcodes according to the following rules 1. LN NLL
#eg N1 1AA 2. LLN NLL eg SW4 0QL 3. LNN NLL eg M23 4PJ 4. LLNN NLL
#eg WS14 0JT 5. LLNL NLL eg SW1N 4TB 6. LNL NLL eg W1C 8LQ Thanks
#to Simon Bell for informin ...
zip=^[a-zA-Z]{1,2}[0-9][0-9A-Za-z]{0,1} {0,1}[0-9][A-Za-z]{2}$

#This regular expression matches dates of the form XX/XX/YYYY
#where XX can be 1 or 2 digits long and YYYY is always 4
#digits long.
dates=^\d{1,2}\/\d{1,2}\/\d{4}$
```

Thus, to extract a regex pattern, you would simply write the following code:

```
String regex =getRegex("regexCache.txt","email");
```

You'll notice that the data cache file also allows comments. You'll find these particularly useful as you drift away from the details of the pattern itself after having written it.

Finally, it should be noted that there are several different and valid approaches to take here. One approach would be to subclass the Properties file for yourself and offer a regex-friendly implementation. In the future, I wouldn't be surprised if Sun decided to do something like this or offer some other convenience mechanism for extracting regex patterns from a file without requiring that the regex be Java-delimited. In the meantime, Listing 4-8 provides a read-only implementation of a custom property file reader that allows regex patterns to be stored without being double delimited.

Listing 4-8. Custom Property File Reader

```
01  import java.util.Properties;
02  import java.util.regex.*;
03  import java.util.*;
04  import java.io.*;
05  import java.nio.*;
06  import java.nio.channels.*;
07  import java.util.logging.Logger;

08  /**
09   * Provides a read-only extension of the java.util.properties file.
10   * This class is unique because it is especially designed to read in
11   * regular expressions that are not double delimited, as the String
12   * class requires. Thus, \s is the actual string used to represent a
13   * whitespace character, not \\s. Accordingly, this class does not allow
14   * the regex patterns to be modified programmatically, nor does it
15   * follow the normal property file convention for \n,\t, etc., or
16   * multiline properties. Please see the documentation for the
17   * load method
18   */
19  public class RegexProperties extends Properties{
20      private static Logger log = Logger.getAnonymousLogger();
21      /**
22       * See load(FileInputStream inStream)
23       *
24       * @param String the name of the file to load
25       * @throws IOException if there's an IO problem
26       * @throws  PatternSyntaxException if the File format isn't properly
27       * formed, per the specification given above.
28       */

29      public void load(String inStream)
30      throws IOException, PatternSyntaxException{
31          load(new FileInputStream(inStream));
32      }
33      /**
34       * Specialized property file for reading regular expressions
35       * stored as properties. Reads a property list (key and
36       * element pairs) from the input stream using a FileChannel,
37       * thus allowing the usage of all characters. The stream is
38       * assumed to be using the ISO 8859-1 character encoding.
39       * Every property occupies one line of the input stream. Each
40       * line is terminated by a line terminator (\n or \r or \r\n).
```

```
41     * The entire contents of the file are read in.
42     *
43     * A line that contains only whitespace or whose first
44     * nonwhitespace character is an ASCII # or ! is ignored
45     * (thus, # or ! indicate comment lines).
46     *
47     * Every line other than a blank line or a comment line describes
48     * one property to be added to the table. The key consists of
49     * all the characters in the line starting with the first
50     * nonwhitespace character and up to, but not including,
51     * the first ASCII =, :, or whitespace character. Any whitespace
52     * after the key is skipped; if the first nonwhitespace character
53     * after the key is = or :, then it is ignored. Whitespace characters
54     * after the = or ; are <B>not</B> skipped, and become part of the
55     * value. This is a deliberate change from the default behavior of
56     * the class, in order to support regular expressions, which may very
57     * well need those characters. All remaining characters on the line
58     * become part of the associated element string. If the last
59     * character on the line is \, then the next line is <B>not </B>
60     * treated as a continuation of the current line. Again, this is a
61     * deliberate change from the default behavior of the class, in
62     * order to support regular expressions.
63     *
64     * @param FileInputStream inStream the actual property file
65     * @throws IOException if there's an IO problem
66     * @throws  PatternSyntaxException if the File format isn't properly
67     * formed, per the specification given above.
68     */

69     public void load(FileInputStream inStream)
       throws IOException, PatternSyntaxException{
70     // load the contents of the file
71     FileChannel fc = inStream.getChannel();

72     ByteBuffer bb = ByteBuffer.allocate((int)fc.size());
73     fc.read(bb);
74     bb.flip();
75     String fileContent = new String(bb.array());

76     //define a pattern that breaks the contents down line by line
77     Pattern pattern = Pattern.compile("^(.*)$",Pattern.MULTILINE);
78     Matcher matcher = pattern.matcher(fileContent);

79     //iterate through the fileContent, line by line
```

```
80    while (matcher.find()){
81        //extract the relevant part of each file.
82        //in this case, relevant means the characters
83        //between the beginning of the line and its end
84        String line = matcher.group(1) ;

85        //if the line is null or a comment, ignore it
86        if (
87            line != null &&
88            !"".equals(line.trim()) &&
89            !line.startsWith("#") &&
90            !line.startsWith("!")
91        )
92        {
93            String keyValue[] = null;

94            //was the key value entry split with the '='
95            //character or the ':' character? Both are legal.
96            if (line.indexOf("=") > 0  )
97              keyValue = line.split("=",2);
98            else
99              keyValue = line.split(":",2);

100           //final check that keyValue isn't null, because we
101           //are going to be entering into a map and trimming it
102           if (keyValue != null)
103           {
104               super.put(keyValue[0].trim(),keyValue[1]);
105           }
106       }
107   }

108   fc = null;
109   bb = null;
110   }
111   /**
112    *
113    * Not supported. This is designed to be a read-only class
114    * only. Throws UnsupportedOperationException.
115    * @param String the key to be placed into this property
116    * list.
117    * @param  String the value corresponding to key.
118    * @throws UnsupportedOperationException
119    *
120    */
```

```
121     public void store(FileOutputStream out, String header)
122     throws UnsupportedOperationException
123     {
124         String msg = "unsupported for this class";
125         throw new UnsupportedOperationException(msg);
126     }
127     /**!
128      * Not supported.
129      * @param Object t - Mappings to be stored in this map.
130      *
131      * @returns nothing, since this call always throws an
132      * UnsupportedOperationException.
133      * @throws  UnsupportedOperationException
134      */
135     public void putAll(Map t)
136     {
137         String msg = "unsupported for this class";
138         throw new UnsupportedOperationException(msg);
139     }
140}
```

Compile Your Patterns As You Need To

Make a point of compiling your Patterns on a just-in-time basis if there's a chance you won't need them. That is, don't compile a Pattern object until the time you actually need it, *if* you actually need it. This is especially true in a logically branching method, in which there might not be any need to even use a Pattern. Better yet, *look* for opportunities to conditionally compile your patterns.

For example, say you're parsing log entries in your log Handler, because you want to send out an emergency e-mail if any of the entries contain an Exception. Of course, you could compile the pattern *(.*Exception)* and check it against every String that's logged. However, this is probably overkill, because you don't, of course, expect any exceptions in your code. It's probably a better idea to simply do a String.indexOf for the substring *Exception* and only try the extraction process if the index is positive. This is demonstrated in Listing 4-9.

Listing 4-9. Log Handler That Checks for Exceptions

```java
import java.util.logging.*;
import java.util.regex.*;
/**
 * Listens for exceptions in the log entries
 * @author M Habibi
 */
public class ExceptionHandler extends StreamHandler{

    /**
     * examines the record being logged, and checks to see if
     * it contains an exception
     * @param record the LogRecord about to be logged
     */
    public void publish(LogRecord record){
        //extract the message
        String msg = record.getMessage();

        //check to see if the message contains an exception
        int exceptionIndex = msg.indexOf("Exception");

        //if the message didn't contains the String
        //'Exception', then don't bother compiling the regex
        if (exceptionIndex > -1){

            Pattern pattern =
              Pattern.compile("(.*Exception.*)");

            Matcher matcher = pattern.matcher(msg);

            if (matcher != null && matcher.find()){
                String err = "EXCEPTION FOUND " + matcher.group(1);
              System.out.println(err);
              //put emailer here
            }
        }
    }
}
```

This isn't particularly clever code, but it does a good job of cultivating those suspects that require further investigation and those that can't possibly be candidates. The principle here, of course, is intelligent discrimination. If you're able to rule out impossible candidates, then you'll save time and resources in production. Listing 4-10 shows the test harness.

Listing 4-10. Adding the Log Handler to Your Log

```java
import java.util.logging.*;

/**
* Demonstrates the usage of the log listener
*/
public class LogDemo{
    public static void main(String args[]){
        Logger log = Logger.global;
        setLoggerhandler(log);

        //test the code. Do even finest-grade entries get
        //logged?
        log.finest(new Exception().toString());
    }

    /**
    * Sets a logger handler for the given log.
    * @param log the logger that needs an listener
    * @version 1.0 5/12/2002
    */
    public static void setLoggerhandler(Logger logger){
        Handler handler = new ExceptionHandler();
        logger.addHandler(handler);

        //set to handle all errors, so that it will examine
        //all errors.
        logger.setLevel(Level.ALL);
    }}
```

> **NOTE** You'll notice that this code doesn't deal with the `Logger.throwing` method, and it doesn't actually send out an e-mail. Don't worry, code that does is provided at http://www.influxs.com. However, the implementation here would require explanations that are beyond the scope of regular expressions.

Don't Limit Yourself to a Regex Solution

When you have a hammer, everything starts to look like a nail. It's important to be aware that not all text-parsing problems require a regex solution. For example, say you need to break a comma-delimited String into its various components. Of course, it's easy enough to write a regex that does this. However, you don't need regular expressions for this problem; the StringTokenizer is enough.

Along the same lines, you don't have to limit yourself exclusively to a regex or a traditional Java solution; you can mix and match. For example, say you need to parse a log file and identify the type and frequency of the Exceptions in it. You could probably write a regex that does this for you in a single line—I'm not smart or patient enough to do this, but there are probably plenty of people who are.

However, I would contend that this probably isn't the correct approach in Java. By the time you're done writing, testing, and documenting the regex, the other programmers on your team will be trembling in fear at the thought of maintaining your code. It's probably easier to take a programmatic solution that takes advantage of regular expressions, as opposed to writing a pure regex solution. Such a solution is presented in Listing 4-9.

The code in Listing 4-11 is self-sufficient and should be ready to go as is. However, it requires two small accommodations. First, you'll have to define a regexCache.txt file to hold your regex pattern, as discussed previously for Listing 4-7. Second, you'll have to define a regex entry in that file for the key *exRegex*. The value of the entry should be *\s([a-zA-Z.]*\.[a-zA-Z.]*Exception)*. Then, to run the code, you simply have to point to a log file that contains exceptions.

Listing 4-11. The Log Parser

```java
import java.util.regex.*;
import java.util.*;
import java.io.*;
import java.nio.*;
import java.nio.channels.*;
import java.beans.*;

/**
* This class parses the log, and identifies all of the
* exceptions thrown, as well as the frequency with which
* they occurred.
*
*@ author M Habibi
*/
public class LogParser{
```

```
/**
* the key of the regex that applies the exception
* pattern
*/
public static final String REGEX_KEY="exRegex";

/**
* The name of the file that contains the regex keys.
* This should probably be extracted from a properties file,
* but we'll leave it as is for right now.
*/
public static final String REGEX_KEY_FILE="regexCache.txt";

/**
* Runs the program from the command line.
* @param args[]. If the name of the log file
* is passed in, then it is used. Otherwise,
* the code looks for a file name 'server.log'
*/
public static void main(String args[]){
    String logFile = "server.log";
    if (args != null && args.length == 1){
        logFile = args[0];
    }
    examineLog(logFile);

}

/**
* parses the log, and identifies all of the
* exceptions thrown, as well as the frequency with which
* they occurred.
*
* @param logFile the name of the log file to examine.
* @param regexCacheFile the name of the file containing
* the regex cache.
* @param regexKey the name of the file containing the
* key in the regecCacheFile.
* @return a Map containing the names of the exceptions
* found as keys, and their frequency as values
*/
```

```java
public static Map examineLog(
    String logFile,
    String regexCacheFile,
    String regexKey){
     //create a map that will preserve the order of the
     //exceptions as they occur
     Map retval = new LinkedHashMap();

     //extract the regex
     String regex  =getRegex(regexCacheFile,regexKey);

     //get the contents of the log file
     String fileContent = readFile(logFile);

     //compile the pattern, and mark the time
     //for its execution
     Pattern pattern =
        Pattern.compile(regex, Pattern.MULTILINE);

     long startTime = System.currentTimeMillis() ;
     Matcher matcher = pattern.matcher(fileContent);

     //seek out matches.
     while (matcher.find()){
        String exceptionName = matcher.group(1);
        incrementMapCount(retval,exceptionName);
     }

     long endTime = System.currentTimeMillis() ;
     long totalTime= endTime - startTime;

     //record the total processing time
     totalTime =totalTime/(long)1000;
     System.out.println("totalTime = " + totalTime);

     //display the output
     System.out.println("retval = " + retval);

     return retval;


    }
```

```
/**
* parses the log, and identifies all of the
* exceptions thrown, as well as the frequency with which
* they occurred.
*
* @param logFile the name of the log file to examine
* @return a Map containing the names of the exceptions
* found as keys, and their frequency as values
*/
public static Map examineLog(String logFile){
    Map map =examineLog(logFile,REGEX_KEY_FILE,REGEX_KEY);
    return map;
}


/**
* Extracts the contents of the given file at the given key.
* This particular extraction process is specifically
* expecting the content of the file to be a
* non-Java-delimited regex pattern.
*
* @param fileName the name of the file that
* has the regex pattern.
* @param key the key that defines the regex in the file
* @returns a string holding the content of the file
* @author Mehran Habibi
**/
private static String getRegex(String fileName, String key){
 String retval = null;

 //get content of the file
 String content = readFile(fileName);

 //if the file has content, then try to find the key
 if (content != null)
 {
  //look for a beginning of line, followed by the key,
  //followed by an equal sign, and capture everything between
  //that key and the end of the line.
  String keyRegex = "^"+key+"=(.*)$";
  Pattern pattern = Pattern.compile(keyRegex,Pattern.MULTILINE);

  Matcher matcher = pattern.matcher(content);
```

```java
    if (matcher != null && matcher.find())
        retval = matcher.group(1);


}


return retval;
}


/**
 * Increments the count of the exception name, or creates
 * a new entry for it.
 * @param map the map expected to hold String keys of the
 * exception name, and Integer values to track the count.
 * @param exceptionName the name of the exception being
 * tracked
 */
private static void incrementMapCount
(Map map, String exceptionName)
{
    Integer currentCount = (Integer)map.get(exceptionName);

    if (currentCount == null){
        map.put(exceptionName, new Integer(1));

    }
    else{
        currentCount = new Integer(currentCount.intValue() + 1);
        map.put(exceptionName,currentCount);

    }

}

/**
*Returns the content of the file in question as string.
* @param fileName the name of the file in question
* @return A string containing the file's content
*
*/
```

```
private static String readFile(String fileName){
    String retval = null;
    try{
        //open a connection to the file
        FileInputStream fis =
        new FileInputStream(fileName);
        FileChannel fc = fis.getChannel();
        //create a byte buffer big enough
        //to hold the content of the file,
        //and read the file content into it
        ByteBuffer bb = ByteBuffer.allocate((int)fc.size());
        fc.read(bb);
        bb.flip();

        //save the contents as a string
        retval = new String(bb.array());

        //clean up
        fc.close();
        bb= null;
        fis = null;
        fc= null;

    }
    catch(Exception e){
        e.printStackTrace();
    }

    return retval;
    }
}
```

Listing 4-11 is a long example, but it's worthwhile to look over. There's not a lot going on here in terms of regex complexity, but the code does a reasonable job of using a Java-based, code-oriented solution: It's not caught up in being a regex solution. In fact, the regular expressions are treated like simply another tool, much like the Map or the FileChannel. This is, I think, the way it should be.

The Pattern object is conditionally compiled in the examineLog method, the important regex pattern is externalized, and the approach is object oriented and logic based. You don't need to be regex expert to figure what's going on here, which is the point. Incidentally, when I ran it on my 1500 MHz laptop with 256 RAM, it executed in 4 seconds, even though the size of the log was 9.26MB.

Summary

This chapter provided explanations, details, and examples of how to approach regex in Java's objected-oriented environment. I discussed how to access files, covered strategies for optimizing speed by caching file content to memory, explored how and why to store regex patterns externally, and presented strategies for balancing regex code with natural object-oriented programming paradigms. In Chapter 5, you'll use this material, as well as the material presented in the previous chapters, to address real-world regex problems.

FAQs

Q: What does the pattern <((?i)TITLE>)(.*?)</\1 break down to?

A: The answer is given in Table 4-1. Of particular interest is the subgroup *(.*?)*. Notice that this is a reluctant qualifier, thus it will only match as little as possible before seeing the next *<title>* element. The difference here is that given *<title>first title</title><title>second title></title>*, the pattern will only extract *first title*. However, without the reluctant qualifier, it would extract *first title</title><title>second title>*.

Table 4-1. The Pattern <((?i)TITLE>)(.?)</(/1)*

Regex	Description
<	The character < followed by
(	A group consisting of
(?i)	A case-insensitive comparison of
T	The character *T* followed by
I	The character *I* followed by
T	The character *T* followed by
L	The character *L* followed by
E	The character *E* followed by
>	The character >
)	Close group
(	Followed by a group consisting of
.	Any character
*	Repeated any number of times
?	Matched reluctantly
)	Close group, followed by
<	The character < followed by
/	The character / followed by
\1	The first group, which matched *(?i)TITLE>*

* **In English:** Extract the contents of first occurrence of the *TITLE* element and be willing to match any case version of *TITLE*, including *Title*, *title*, and so on.

Q: How do I know if my regex is too complex?

A: The first goal of any regex pattern is, of course, that it works accurately and efficiently enough. The second goal is that it be legible. How do you know if it's legible? My advice is comment it with as much detail as you feel it needs, and then pass it to a few developers who are likely to have to decipher it. If they follow it (or better yet, if they're able to modify it), then it's probably clear enough. If not, then you may want to consider refactoring.

CHAPTER 5

Practical Examples

"I took a speed reading course and read War and Peace in 20 minutes.
It's about Russia."
— Woody Allen

IN THIS CHAPTER, I'll think aloud as I solve several regex problems. This should provide some insight into the process of forming nontrivial regex solutions. Some of these examples are problems that I've found on a regex or Java newsgroup, and others were created for this chapter.

> **NOTE** The problems in this chapter take advantage of the `RegexProperties` class, which was defined in Chapter 4. `RegexProperties` is a class that extends `java.util.Properties` and allows you to load regex patterns from a properties file. The main advantage here is that the patterns don't have to be Java-delimited. Thus, you can actually use \d instead of \\d. For more details on the `RegexProperties` class, please see Chapter 4.

Confirming the Format of a Phone Number

This first example confirms that a given phone number has the normal format for a U.S. phone number.

Before beginning in earnest, I have to make a decision: Do I want to write my own pattern or try to find an existing one? Normally, the first thing I would do is check some online regex resource, such as `http://www.regexlib.com`, to find an existing pattern. However, because this is a relatively simple pattern, and because I want to demonstrate the process of writing it, I'll create it myself.

Because I've decided to write the pattern myself, the first question I need to answer is, what is a phone number? I begin by working backward from some sample numbers. This is the pull technique described in Chapter 1. It requires that I take some actual data and try to pull the pattern out of it. Say my sample set is this:

614-345-6789

345-6789

345 6789

345.6789

3456789

(614)345-6789

6143456789

I pick the first phone number on the list as my pattern model. In examining it, I see a fairly obvious blueprint: three digits, a hyphen, three digits, a hyphen, and then four digits. That leads to the pattern *\d{3}-\d{3}-\d{4}*. Table 5-1 shows the process of deriving the pattern.

Table 5-1. Pulling a General Regex Pattern from 614-345-6789

Step	What I Did	Why I Did It	Justification	Resulting Pattern
Step 1	Nothing	Initial state	N/A	614-345-6789
Step 2	Replaced digits with *\d*	To get a more generic description	*\d* stands for any single digit	\d\d\d-\d\d\d-\d\d\d\d
Step 3	Replaced *\d\d\d* with *\d{3}*	To produce a more succinct pattern	*\d{3}* is exactly equal to *\d\d\d*	\d{3}-\d{3}-\d\d\d\d
Step 4	Replaced *\d\d\d\d* with *\d{4}*	To produce a more succinct pattern	*\d{4}* is exactly equal to *\d\d\d\d*	\d{3}-\d{3}-\d{4}

Of course, the pattern also has to accommodate numbers consisting of only seven digits, such as *345-6789*. At present, it can't, because it's modeled after data that has nine digits. Reconciling the pattern to do so leads to *(?:\d{3}-)?\d{3}-\d{4}*. Table 5-2 shows the process of deriving the pattern.

Table 5-2. Pushing \d{3}-\d{3}-\d{4} to Accommodate Seven-Digit Numbers

Step	What I Did	Why I Did It	Justification	Resulting Pattern
Step 5	Nothing	Initial state	N/A	\d{3}-\d{3}-\d{4}
Step 6	Grouped the leftmost *\d{3}-* in parentheses, producing *(\d{3}-)*	To treat *\d{3}-* as a single entity that might or might not exist.	Any part of a pattern can be subgrouped.	(\d{3}-)\d{3}-\d{4}
Step 7	Made *(\d{3}-)* optional by producing *(\d{3}-)?*	So that users can omit area codes.	Adding *?* after a group makes it optional.	(\d{3}-)?\d{3}-\d{4}
Step 8	Added a *?:* inside the opening *(* of *(\d{3}-)* to produce *(?:\d{3}-)?*	It makes the expression more efficient. Non-capturing groups require less memory.	Adding *?:* inside a group makes the group noncapturing.	(?:\d{3}-)?\d{3}-\d{4}

Now the pattern will accept any seven or ten digit sequence of numbers, as long as they are grouped into sets of threes and fours, and separated by hyphens.

A Brief Digression on Working with Regex in Java

If I were programming in Perl, the next natural step would probably be to account for punctuation in the candidate, deal with an opening parenthesis that might or might not be there, and so on. Of course, this would most likely be addressed in the pattern itself.

But I'm not using Perl; I'm using a full featured, object-oriented language that's been designed to deal with nuisances while remaining clear. I decide to take advantage of that by scrubbing the data, and relying more on programmatic logic and less on regex wizardry.

Next, I use `String.replaceAll` to remove all punctuation and spacing from the phone number, as follows:

```
String scrubbedPhone = phone.replaceAll("\\p{Punct}|\\s","");
```

This replaces any and all punctuation or space characters with a zero-length string.

> **NOTE** *\p{Punct}* is a POSIX, U.S. ASCII predefined class that matches any punctuation character. Specifically, it matches *!"#$%&'()*+,-./:;<=>?@[\]^_`{|}~*. It was introduced in Chapter 1, in Table 1-12.

This way, I can count on the phone number being in the form *6143456789* or *3456789*. This is great news, because I can now simplify the pattern even further, as shown in Table 5-3. By breaking the process down into a separate step, I've decreased the amount of complexity that will go into a given pattern.

Table 5-3. Removing References to - from \d{3}-\d{3}-\d{4} to Accommodate the Data Scrub

Step	What I Did	Why I Did It	Justification	Resulting Pattern
Step 9	Nothing	Initial state	N/A	(?:\d{3}-)?\d{3}-\d{4}
Step 10	Removed all references to the character -	This scrubbing guarantees that I'll never have to deal with punctuation in the phone number. Thus, it would be a mistake to expect it.	Removing the - simply means that the pattern won't check for, or require, the existence of a hyphen.	(?:\d{3})?\d{3}\d{4}
Step 11	Treated *(\d{3})* as a single entity and checked for its existence one or two times; thus, replaced *(?:\d{3})?\d{3}* with *(?:\d{3}){1,2}*	To make the expressions less verbose.	*(?:\d{3})?\d{3}* means "three digits or six digits." *(?:\d{3}){1,2}* means exactly the same thing. Thus, they're logically equivalent statements.	(?:\d{3}){1,2}\d{4}
Step 12	Went back to using the pattern from step 10.	Although the pattern from step 11 is briefer, it's more difficult to read.	See previous.	(?:\d{3})?\d{3}\d{4}

Notice that I back off from a change made in step 11 in step 12. Although it's true that step 11 made the expression less verbose, it also made it more difficult to read. In this case, I'm willing to have the pattern be slightly longer, if it will also be easier to read and maintain. Thus, the heart of my code consists of two lines. The first is line 32, which strips out any and all punctuation from the candidate:

```
String tmp = phone.replaceAll("\\p{Punct}|\\s","");
```

The second is line 36, which applies the pattern:

```
boolean retval = tmp.matches(PHONE_PATTERN) // (\d{3})?\d{3}\d{4}
```

Listing 5-1 shows the full implementation.

Listing 5-1. Searching for a Phone Number

```
01  import java.util.regex.*;
02  import java.util.logging.Logger;

03  public class MatchPhoneNumber{
04      private static Logger log = Logger.getAnonymousLogger();
05      private static final String   PHONE_NUMBER_KEY="phoneNumber";
06      /**
07       * Confirms that the format for the given phone number is valid.
08       * @param phone a String representing the phone number.
09       * @returns true if the phone number format is acceptable.
10       */
11      public static boolean isPhoneValid(String phone){
12          boolean retval=false;
13              String msg = "\r\nCANDIDATE:" + phone;


14          //make sure the candidate has a shot passing
15          if (phone != null && phone.length() > 6)
16          {
17              //load the regex properties file
18              RegexProperties rb = new RegexProperties();
19              try
20              {
21                rb.load("../regex.properties");
22              }
```

```
23          catch(Exception e)
24          {
25                  e.printStackTrace();
26          }

27          //scrub the phone number, removing spaces
28          //and punctuation. We could store this
29          //pattern in the regex.property file as well,
30          //but it's not really so complex that
31          //it's confusing when Java-delimited
32          String tmp = phone.replaceAll("\\p{Punct}|\\s","");

33          //extract appropriate regex pattern and run check
34          //in this case (\d{3})?\d{3}\d{4}
36          String phoneNumberPattern=rb.getProperty(PHONE_NUMBER_KEY);

37          //do the actual comparison
38          retval= tmp.matches(phoneNumberPattern);

39          //log for debug purposes
40          msg += ":\r\nREGEX:" + phoneNumberPattern;
41      }
42     msg += "\r\nRESULT:" + retval +"\r\n";
43     log.info(msg);
44     return retval;
45   }
46  public static void main(String args[]) throws Exception{
47    if (args != null && args.length == 1)
48       System.out.println(isPhoneValid(args[0]));
49    else
50       System.out.println("usage: java MatchPhoneNumber <phoneNumber>");
51   }
52 }
```

Even programmers who don't know anything about regex can follow the code, which speaks to the elegance of J2SE regex.

Is the extra verbosity justified? Would it have been better to simply write the regex in a single line for this particular case? This is the sort of decision you'll need to make on a case-by-case basis for your particular needs. In my opinion, it's better to err on the side of verbosity than to risk terse code.

Confirming Zip Codes

The next challenge is to provide a method that confirms zip codes for the United States. The method needs to accommodate punctuation, a space, or no delimiter at all between the five-digit and four-digit parts of the zip code. It needs to accommodate zip codes that are only five digits long. Suddenly, there's requirements creep: It now needs to validate zip codes for Canada, the United Kingdom, Argentina, Sweden, Japan, and the Netherlands as well.

The first thing I do is search the Web for patterns, starting at http://www.regexlib.com. This returns regular expressions for all of the countries previously mentioned. Next, I take those regular expressions and create entries in the regex.properties file, so I can use the RegexProperties class from Chapter 4.

The point of doing so, of course, is to externalize the expressions themselves and to avoid having to double-delimit special characters. I decide to use intelligent keys for the property keys. That is, I'm anticipating that I'll have access to the country code for each of these regex patterns. Therefore, I can define the property file keys based on that country code. For example, since the country code for Japan is *JP*, I define the key to the zip code pattern for Japan as *zipJP*. Listing 5-2 summarizes the entries made to the regex.properties file.

Listing 5-2. New Entries in the regex.properties File

```
#Japanese postal codes
zipJP=^\d{3}-\d{4}$


#US postal codes
zipUS=^\d{5}\p{Punct}?\s?(?:\d{4})?$


#Dutch postal code
zipNL=^[0-9]{4}\s*[a-zA-Z]{2}$


#Argentinean postal code
zipAR=^\d{3}-\d{4}$


#Swedish postal code
zipSE=^(s-|S-){0,1}[0-9]{3}\s?[0-9]{2}$


#Canadian postal code
zipCA=^([A-Z]\d[A-Z]\s\d[A-Z]\d)$


#UK postal code
zipUK=^[a-zA-Z]{1,2}[0-9][0-9A-Za-z]{0,1} {0,1}[0-9][A-Za-z]{2}$
```

Finally, I write the code. The algorithm is to look up the appropriate regex for a given country given the appropriate country code, apply the pattern, and return true or false as appropriate. Listing 5-3 shows the code that does this.

Listing 5-3. Matching Zip Codes for Various Countries

```
01  import java.io.*;
02  import java.util.logging.Logger;
03  import java.util.regex.*;

04  /**
05  *Validates zip codes from the given country.
06  *@author M Habibi
07  */
08  public class MatchZipCodes{
09      private static Logger log = Logger.getAnonymousLogger();
10      private static final String ZIP_PATTERN="zip";
11      private static RegexProperties regexProperties;
12      //load the regex properties file
13      //do this at the class level
14      static
15      {
16          try
17          {
18              regexProperties = new RegexProperties();
19              regexProperties.load("../regex.properties");
20          }
21          catch(Exception e)
22          {
23              e.printStackTrace();
24          }
25      }

26      public static void main(String args[]){
27          String msg = "usage: java MatchZipCodes countryCode Zip";

28          if (args != null && args.length == 2)
29              msg = ""+isZipValid(args[0],args[1]);

30          //output either the usage message, or the results
31          //of running the isZipValid method
32          System.out.println(msg);
33      }
```

```
34      /**
35       * Confirms that the format for the given zip code is valid.
36       * @param the <code>String</code> countryCode
37       * @param the <code>String</code> zip
38       * @return <code>boolean</code>
39       *
40       * @author M Habibi
41       */
42      public static boolean isZipValid(String countryCode, String zip)
43      {
44          boolean retval=false;
45          //use the country code to form a unique into the regex
46          //properties file
47          String zipPatternKey = ZIP_PATTERN + countryCode.toUpperCase();

48          //extract the regex pattern for the given country code
49          String zipPattern = regexProperties.getProperty(zipPatternKey);

50          //if there was some sort of problem, don't bother trying
51          //to execute the regex
52          if (zipPattern != null)
53              retval = zip.trim().matches(zipPattern);
54          else
55          {
56              String msg = "regex for country code "+countryCode;
57              msg+= " not found in property file ";
58              log.warning(msg);
59          }
60          //create log report
61          String msg = "regex="+zipPattern +
62          "\nzip="+zip+"\nCountryCode="+
63          countryCode+"\nmatch result="+retval;
64          log.finest(msg);

65          return retval;
66      }
67 }
```

Outside of the comments and such, the real work in this method is done in three lines. Line 47 forms the proper key based on the country code:

```
47      String zipPatternKey = ZIP_PATTERN + countryCode.toUpperCase();
```

For example, `zipPatternKey` equals *zipUS* for the *US* country code. Next, line 49 extracts the relevant pattern based on that key:

```
49    String zipPattern = regexProperties.getProperty(zipPatternKey);
```

Line 53 actually compares the pattern against the key:

```
53              retval = zip.trim().matches(zipPattern);
```

The only regex change I made in this example was to make the actual pattern just a little more memory efficient and a little more lenient, as shown in Table 5-4. Specifically, leniency means that the pattern will accept any punctuation, a space, or no delimiter at all between the first five digits and the last four digits of a U.S. zip code. The pattern will also accept five digits as a sufficient U.S. zip code.

Table 5-4. Making the Zip Code Pattern More Lenient and Efficient

Step	What I Did	Why I Did It	Justification	Resulting Pattern
Step 1	Nothing	Initial state	N/A	\d{5}(-\d{4})?
Step 2	Added *?:* inside the capturing group *(-\d{4})* to produce *(?:-\d{4})*	To produce a more efficient pattern.	We don't need a capture here.	\d{5}(?:-\d{4})?
Step 3	Replaced - with *\p{Punct}?* to produce *(?:\p{Punct}?\d{4})?*	Any punctuation—or no punctuation at all—can be used as a delimiter.	*\p{Punct}?* is a superset of -, and it's optional, so the regex engine is now willing to accept any punctuation or no punctuation at all as a delimiter.	\d{5}(?:\p{Punct}?\d{4})?

Table 5-4. Making the Zip Code Pattern More Lenient and Efficient (Continued)

Step	What I Did	Why I Did It	Justification	Resulting Pattern
Step 4	Added a *\s?* pattern to the list of acceptable delimiters between the five digits and the four digits of a U.S. zip code	Zip codes that use a space or empty string to separate the five digits from the four digits will pass.	A space between the five digits of a U.S. zip code and the following four digits is optional. This is simply a more lenient interpretation.	\d{5}(?:\p{Punct}?\s?\d{4})?
Step 5	Moved the *\p{Punct}?\s?* out of the noncapturing group	This improves readability. Optional subpatterns inside a optional noncapturing group can be hard to follow.	Logically, the two are equivalent.	\d{5}\p{Punct}?\s?(?:\d{4})?
Step 6	Surrounded the pattern with a beginning-of-line ^ tag and an end-of-line $ tag	This increases matching speed. The more precise the pattern, the better it will perform.	All zip codes will be coming into the method as extracted strings. Thus, they'll always have a beginning of line and an end of line.	^\d{5}\p{Punct}?\s?(?:\d{4})?$

Because the regex patterns are externalized, they can be tweaked later to become more accommodating for the various regions. Better yet, more country codes can be added without requiring code changes: Simply add the appropriate entries to the `regex.properties` file.

The point here is that even using generic regex patterns found online, I still have a very Java-like flavor to the code. It's modular, adaptable, scalable, and clear.

Confirming Date Formats

In this example, I need a method that will validate a date format. The requirements are very explicit. Some sort of punctuation between the various date tokens is required, and a space isn't considered punctuation. The method should accept either two digits or four digits for the year, and either one or two digits for the day and month. I also need to make sure the date isn't in the future. I can expect the first date token to be the month, the second date token to be the day of that month, and the last date token to be the year. Thus, valid entries might be as follows:

11/30/2002

4/25/03

03-29/2003

11/30/1902

2/25-03

06#9/2003

Again, the first thing to do is search the Web. I find a few patterns that might work here. The first follows, and it's described as being very robust, dealing with leap years, and so on: *^(?:(?:(?:0?[13578]|1[02])(\/|-|\.)31)\1|(?:(?:0?[1,3-9]|1[0-2])(\/|-|\.)(?:29|30)\2))(?:(?:1[6-9]|[2-9]\d)?\d{2})$|^(?:0?2(\/|-|\.)29\3(?:(?:(?:1[6-9]|[2-9]\d)?(?:0[48]|[2468][048]|[13579][26])|(?:(?:16|[2468][048]|[3579][26])00))))$|^(?:(?:0?[1-9])|(?:1[0-2]))(\/|-|\.)(?:0?[1-9]|1\d|2[0-8])\4(?:(?:1[6-9]|[2-9]\d)?\d{2})$.*

I decide to pass on it for now.

The second pattern I find is *^\d{1,2}\/\d{1,2}\/\d{4}$*, which looks promising, but limits itself to four-digit years. It could work, but I would have to tweak it. Next, I come across *((\d{2})|(\d))\/((\d{2})|(\d))\/((\d{4})|(\d{2}))*. At first glance, it looks like I might have to pull the second pattern toward the third.

I don't like the third pattern as is, because it uses a lot capturing groups that it doesn't really need. Noncapturing groups would do as well, and they would be more efficient. This immediately makes me a little suspicious. It's also more verbose than I had hoped for. Of course, it's possible that the verbose nature of the expression makes it more efficient, but I doubt that an author who was worried about efficiency would have left all of those useless capturing groups in there.

Whichever pattern I choose, I'll probably want to replace any and all punctuation within the candidate string with a character that's easy to work with. I would just get rid of all punctuation, but then I wouldn't know if a date such as *1111971* was referring to January 11, 1971, or November 1, 1971. Thus, I'm going to need a line of code like this:

```
String scrubbedDate = date.replaceAll("\\p{Punct}","@");
```

Here, I'll probably use the @ symbol as a replacement delimiter. It doesn't have any sort of special regex meaning, so it's easier to work with. Next, I'll need to write a pattern to capture the month, day, and year, and make sure that it constitutes a valid date.

Wait a minute—I wonder if there's an easier way. What if I used the `String.split` method around the punctuation and extracted the date from the remaining digits? Then I could just use straight Java code to validate the actual date. To do that, I'll need something like this:

```
String[] datetokens = date.split("\\p{Punct}");
```

This looks fairly easy, so I go with it.

My algorithm becomes the following: Split the date along punctuation marks, use it to create a `Calendar` object, compare that to today, and return true if the `Calendar` object is less than or equal to today. I can write the preliminary method signature as follows:

```
public static boolean isDateValid(String date)
```

Figure 5-1 shows the algorithm.

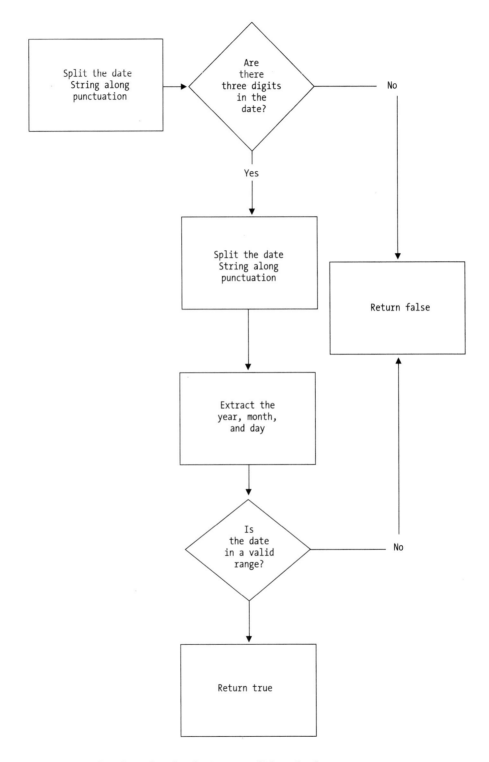

Figure 5-1. The algorithm for the isDateValid method

Listing 5-4 presents the full implementation.

Listing 5-4. Validating a Date

```
01 import java.util.regex.*;
02 import java.io.*;
03 import java.util.logging.Logger;
04 import java.util.GregorianCalendar;
05 import java.util.Calendar;

06 /**
07 *matches dates
08 */
09 public class MatchDates{
10 private static final String DATE_PATTERN = "date";
11 private static final String PROP_FILE = "../regex.properties";
12 private static Logger log = Logger.getAnonymousLogger();
13 public static int LOWER_YEAR_LIMIT = -120;

14    public static void main(String args[]) throws Exception{
15       if (args != null && args.length==1)
16       {
17          boolean b =isDateValid(args[0]);
18          log.info(""+b);
19       }
20       else
21       {
22          System.out.println("usage: java MatchDates dd/dd/dddd");
23       }
24    }

25    /**
26     * Confirms that given date format consists of one or two digits
27     * followed by a punctuation, followed by one or two digits
28     * followed by a punctuation, followed by two or four digits. Further,
29     * it actually validates that the date is less then today, and
30     * and not more then <CODE>LOWER_YEAR_LIMIT</CODE> =120 years in
31     * the past. This method even takes leap years and such into account
32     * @param the <code>String</code> date to be consider
33     * @return <code>boolean</code> true if
34     *
```

```
35    * @author M Habibi
36    */


37    public static boolean isDateValid(String date)
38    {
39      boolean retval=false;
40      date = date.trim();

41      //does the candidate have three digits? Otherwise
42      //the month, day, and year extraction below could
43      //throw a number format exception.
44      boolean hasThreeDigitSections =
45       date.matches("\\d+\\p{Punct}\\d+\\p{Punct}\\d+");

46      if (hasThreeDigitSections)
47      {
48         String[] dateTokens = date.split("\\p{Punct}");

49         if (dateTokens.length == 3)
50         {
51          //Java months are zero based, so subtract 1
52          int month = Integer.parseInt(dateTokens[0]) -1;

53          int day = Integer.parseInt(dateTokens[1]);
54          int year = Integer.parseInt(dateTokens[2]);

55          //in case a 2 digit year was entered
56          if (year < 100)
57            year += 2000;

58          //get boundary years
59          GregorianCalendar today = new GregorianCalendar();
60          //get a lowerLimit that is LOWER_YEAR_LIMIT less then
61          //today
62          GregorianCalendar lowerLimit = new GregorianCalendar();
63          lowerLimit.add(Calendar.YEAR, LOWER_YEAR_LIMIT);

64          //create a candidate representing the proposed date.
65          GregorianCalendar candidate =
66          new GregorianCalendar(year, month,day);
```

```
67          //check the validity of the date
68          if
69          (
70             candidate.before(today)
71           &&
72             candidate.after(lowerLimit)
73           &&//month could be off, say the user entered 55
74             month == candidate.get(Calendar.MONTH)
75           &&//day could be off, say the user entered 55
76             day == candidate.get(Calendar.DAY_OF_MONTH)
77          )
78          {
79              retval = true;
80          }
81       }
82       }
83       return retval;
84    }
85 }
```

The previous example deferred almost all of the heavy lifting to regular expressions. The code in Listing 5-4 uses regex for the split method. Otherwise, it's fairly conventional Java code. This doesn't mean the regex contribution is trivial—as a matter of fact, I would say it's critical. However, once the split method's regex contribution is assimilated, you're back in the comfortable world of Java.

Searching a String

This example searches a given string for the existence of a pattern and returns all of the matching strings. This is very easy code, but it's such a useful little program that it's worthwhile to demonstrate it.

First, I need to decide exactly what I mean by "return." Return what? In this case, I decide to return an ArrayList of matching Strings, because I want the Strings to be in the order in which they were found, and an ArrayList maintains the order in which elements were inserted. Also, I like the idea of returning a well-defined data structure, in case the client wants to, say, step through that structure and examine the data further.

I also decide that I want the client to be able to pass in Pattern.compile flags such as Pattern.MULTILINE and Pattern.DOTALL. It doesn't really cost me anything in the way of additional complexity, and it's a nice feature for the client. At this point, it's worthwhile to get a preliminary method signature written down. I come up with this:

```
    public static ArrayList searchString(
        String content, String searchPattern, int flags
    ) throws IOException
```

Now I'm ready to start writing my method. My first pass looks like Listing 5-5.

Listing 5-5. First Pass at the searchString Method

```
01      public static ArrayList searchString(
02          String content,
03          String searchPattern,
04          int flags
05      )
06      throws IOException
07      {
08          ArrayList retval = new ArrayList();
09          Pattern pattern = null;

10          //compile the pattern
11          if (flags > -1 )
12          {
13              pattern = Pattern.compile(searchPattern, flags);
14          }
15          else
16          {
17              pattern = Pattern.compile(searchPattern);
18          }

19          //extract the matcher for the pattern
20          Matcher matcher = pattern.matcher(content);

21          //iterate through all of the matches, and add
22          //all relevant ones to the arrayList
23          while (matcher.find())
24          {
25              //extract the match and its position
26              String tmp = matcher.group();
27              //insert the matching string
28              //into the map.
29              retval.add(+ tmp);
30          }

32          return retval;
32      }
```

Listing 5-5 isn't terrible. It finds all the relevant matching substrings and returns them in order. I run a few sample tests and find that it works as expected. But it does leave something to be desired. It doesn't really tell me where the string was found, and it might be nice if it were overloaded, so the client isn't forced to pass in a flag if they don't need one.

I decide that for this generation, the client can live without the overloading. However, I do think the client has a right to ask for the position at which the matching strings were found. Thus, I modify the code so that it returns a Map. The Map will contain a key/value pair, which will use the byte position of each find (stored as a String or an Integer—I haven't decided which yet) and the matching substring as a value. Modifying the code, I come up with Listing 5-6. The only significant changes are on lines 7, 25, and 29. By the way, I decided to use a LinkedHashMap on line 8, because I wanted to preserve the order in which the matching Strings were found. A LinkedHashMap is a J2SE 1.4 addition to the Map family that preserves the insertion order of elements.

Listing 5-6. Modified searchString Method Belonging in the RegexUtil Class

```
01   public static Map searchString(
02        String content,
03        String searchPattern,
04        int flags
05   )

06   {
07        Map retval = new LinkedHashMap();
08        Pattern pattern = null;

09        //compile the pattern
10        if (flags > -1 )
11        {
12            pattern = Pattern.compile(searchPattern, flags);
13        }
14        else
15        {
16            pattern = Pattern.compile(searchPattern);
17        }

18        //extract the matcher for the pattern
19        Matcher matcher = pattern.matcher(content);
```

```
20      //iterate through all of the matches, and add
21      //all relevant ones to the arrayList
22      while (matcher.find())
23      {
24          //extract the match and its position
25          int position = matcher.start();
26          String tmp = matcher.group();
27          //insert the matching string and position
28          //into the map.
29          retval.put(position+"",tmp);
30      }

31      return retval;
32 }
```

I decide to make the position a String, to make dealing with the output easier. I don't want to require the client to handle the keys too carefully, so Strings will do for now.

Searching a File

Building on the previous example, I decide to provide a utility for searching the content of a file and returning all matching strings within that file. I'll use FileChannels for the actual file I/O. Although a discussion of FileChannels is beyond the scope of this book, in my opinion they're the best way to access files in Java.

My strategy is to use a FileChannel to open a file, read its content into a String, release the FileChannel, and then use the searchString method to parse the String. This is faster than reading through the file line by line and examining its content, though it is memory intensive. Listing 5-7 shows the code for doing this.

Listing 5-7. Reading in File Content

```
01      /**
02       * extracts the content of a file
03       * @param String fileName the name of the file to extract
04       * @throws IOException
05       *
06       * @return String representing the contents of the file
07       */
08      public static String getFileContent(String fileName)
09      throws IOException{
10          String retval = null;
```

```
11        //get access to the FileChannel
12        FileInputStream fis =
13          new FileInputStream(fileName);
14        FileChannel fc = fis.getChannel();

15        //get the file content
16        retval = getFileContent(fc);

17        //close up shop
18        fc.close();
19        fc = null;

20        return retval;
21     }

22     /**
23      * extracts the content of a file
24      * @param String fileName the name of the file to extract
25      * @throws IOException
26      *
27      * @return String representing the contents of the file
28      */
29     private static String getFileContent(FileChannel fc)
30     throws IOException{
31         String retval = null;
32       //read the contents of the FileChannel
33         ByteBuffer bb = ByteBuffer.allocate((int)fc.size());
34         fc.read(bb);

35         //save the contents as a string
36         bb.flip();
37         retval = new String(bb.array());
38         bb = null;

39         return retval;
40     }
```

Next, I need to provide a method that will load the file, search it, and return the results. Given the two previous methods, this becomes fairly easy, as shown in Listing 5-8.

Listing 5-8. Opening a File, Searching the File, and Returning the Results

```
01     public static Map searchFile(
02         String file,
03         String searchPattern,
04         int flags
05     ) throws IOException
06     {
07         String fileContent = getFileContent(file);
08         Map retval = searchFile(fileContent,searchPattern,flags);
09         return retval;
10     }}
```

I take the program out for a spin and compare it to grep. To be honest, it seems to lack a bit in the comparison. The grep program returns the entire line of a matching token, whereas this method only returns the matching token. That's not terrible, because the client could request the entire line by using the correct regex pattern. But it's not really as friendly as it could be, especially for the average user.

I decide to "pad" the pattern to capture an entire line, assuming that the original search pattern has no punctuation, and thus no regex, in it. Listing 5-9 shows my modified searchFile method.

Listing 5-9. Modifying the searchFile Method to Make It Friendlier

```
01  public static Map searchFile(
02      String file,
03      String searchPattern,
04      int flags
05  ) throws IOException
06  {
07      String fileContent = getFileContent(file);

08      //if the search pattern doesn't have any punctuation
09      //then assume it's not a regular expression and extract
10      //the entire line in which it was found
11      String[] regexTokens = searchPattern.split("\\p{Punct}");

12      if (regexTokens.length == 1)
13      {
14          searchPattern  = "^.*"+ searchPattern+".*$";
15      }

16      Map retval = searchString(fileContent,searchPattern,flags);
17      return retval;
18  }
```

Discussion Point

At this point, there should be some reasonable questions on your mind. Isn't this supposed to be a regex book? There wasn't anything particularly regex-like about the search file and search string methods; they were pretty much straight Java code, which you already know how to write. What's going on?

The point here is that regex is just a tool. It doesn't change the fact that you're still writing Java code, and you need to follow good, modular, object-oriented principles, even as you're working with regular expressions. Regex allows you to bridge trouble spots you might never have crossed otherwise, but it's just a tool. Like any well-built engine, the `java.util.regex` engine announces its excellence by humming quietly along and *not* forcing you to worry about it.

Working with Very Large Files

Another valid question at this point is, what if the content of the file you're trying to parse is too large to make reading all of it into memory a practical option? In general, you have two paths you can take here. You can use one of the new Java features, such as `MappedByteBuffers`, or you can split the file into manageable sections and parse each of those in turn.

If you decide to use `MappedByteBuffers` for regex, Listing 5-10 contains an example showing how. I'm hesitant, however, to advocate `MappedByteBuffers` with regex too strongly for three reasons. First and foremost, their behavior is very system dependent, so you should probably rule them out if you need platform independence. Second, even within a given platform, their behavior isn't well defined. Thus, depending on what else you're doing with your operating system, you could get inconsistent results. Third, you need to consider the fact that, if the entire file can't be loaded into memory at one time, trying to apply a pattern that might have wildcards in it is going to be a tricky affair.

You may very well need to reconsider your patterns, and break the file up into logical blocks based on your insight into its structure. One strategy might be to check the size of the file and divide that by 10, 100, or whatever fraction is easily loadable given your system's memory limitations, and then search that portion. Although this isn't ideal, it is more predictable than the corresponding mapped-memory approach. The bottom line is that regardless of the regex flavor or provider you use, very large files require special treatment.

Listing 5-10. Accessing a File Through a MappedByteBuffer

```
01   public static boolean getFileContentUsingMappedByteBuffer
02   (
03       String fileName
04   ) throws IOException
05   {
06       boolean retval = false;
07       RandomAccessFile raf = new RandomAccessFile(fileName,"rwd");
08       FileChannel fc = raf.getChannel();

09       MappedByteBuffer mbb =
10        fc.map(FileChannel.MapMode.READ_WRITE,0,fc.size());

11       CharSequence cb = mbb.asCharBuffer();

12       return retval;
13   }
```

Modifying the Contents of a File

Now I want to provide a facility that modifies the content of a file based on a regex pattern. That is, I want to provide a mechanism that opens a file, searches its contents based on a regex pattern, and changes every occurrence of that pattern with a replacement string. Because I already have code that will open and search a file, modifying the content of the file is fairly easy. The logic for doing so is shown in Figure 5-2.

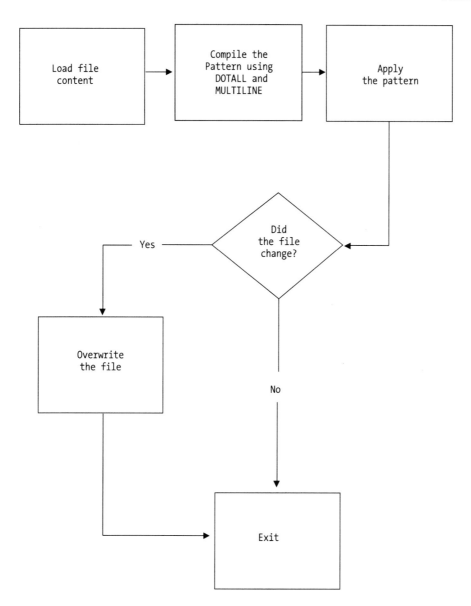

Figure 5-2. Basic flow diagram for updating the content of a file

Again, I decide to use a FileChannel for efficiency, as shown in Listing 5-11.

Listing 5-11. Modifying the Content of a File Based on a Regex Pattern

```
01  /**
02   * updates the content of the file. By default, the
03   * Pattern.MULTILINE is used. Also supports the
04   * $d notation in the replacement string, per the
05   * Matcher.replaceAll method
06   * @param the String fileName is the name and file path
07   * @param the String regex pattern to look for
08   * @param the String replacement for the regex
09   * @throws IOException if there is an IO error
10   *
11   * @return boolean true if the file was updated
12   */
13  public static boolean updateFileContent
14  (
15      String fileName,
16      String regex,
17      String replacement
18  ) throws IOException
19  {
20      boolean retval = false;

21      RandomAccessFile raf =
22          new RandomAccessFile(fileName,"rwd");
23      FileChannel fc = raf.getChannel();

24      String fileContent = getFileContent(fc);
25      //Activate the MULTILINE flag for this regex
26      regex = "(?m)"+regex;

27      String newFileContent =
28          fileContent.replaceAll(regex,replacement);

29      //if nothing changed, then don't update the file
30      if (!newFileContent.equals(fileContent))
31      {
32          setFileContent(newFileContent,fc);
33          retval = true;
34      }
```

```
35    //close up shop
36    fc.close();
37    fc = null;
38    raf = null;

39    return retval;
40  }


41  /**
42   * sets the content of a file. Completely
43   * overwrites previous file content, and truncates
44   * file to the length of the new content.
45   * @param the <code>String</code> newContent
46   * @param the <code>FileChannel</code> fc
47   * @throws <code>IOException</code>
48   *
49   * @author M Habibi
50   */
51  private static void setFileContent(
52      String newContent, FileChannel fc
53  )
54  throws IOException{
55      //write out the content to the file
56      ByteBuffer bb = ByteBuffer.wrap(newContent.getBytes());
57      //truncate the size of the file, in case the
58      //original file content was longer the new
59      //content
60      fc.truncate(newContent.length());

61      //start writing as position 0
62      fc.position(0);
63      fc.write(bb);

64      fc.close();
65      fc = null;
66  }
```

Listing 5-11 takes advantage of the getFileContent method defined earlier in line 29 of Listing 5-7. Otherwise, the example is self-contained.

Extracting Phone Numbers from a File

In this example, I want to parse a file and extract any and all phone numbers. This is a program I wrote to help a friend who owns a small IT shop. He had all sorts of electronic documents and needed to extract phone numbers from them to call his clients back. I'll start this process at the very beginning, where I extracted requirements:

Question: Are you looking for U.S. numbers or international ones?

Answer: U.S. numbers, but that could change.

Q: Is speed an issue? Is someone going to be tapping his foot, waiting for this to finish?

A: No, running overnight is fine.

Q: Do the phone numbers follow any sort of consistent format?

A: They're either seven or ten digits.

Q: Do they have hyphens or spaces in them?

A: It depends—sometimes they do.

Q: Is the format of the file subject to change?

A: Yes.

Q: If there had to be a mistake, would you prefer too many phone number candidates or too few?

A: Too many.

Q: Do you need these numbers returned in any particular kind of format?

A: I hadn't thought of that, but a consistent format would be great.

Q: Do you have some files you've already looked through that I can use for testing?

A: Yes.

Q: How big are these files?

A: Not that big. I don't know.

Q: How many files are there?

A: About ten per night.

Q: What types of files are these?

A: Microsoft Word documents.

I think I have enough information at this point to get started. It sounds like the client wants anything that might be a seven- or ten-digit phone number, and that speed isn't an issue. It also sounds like the files don't get that large. This should be as simple as defining a phone number pattern and using the previously presented search methods. After all, I can already access a file and search its content. I decide to keep the actual regex in a external property file, of course, so I can tweak it as I need to. This is going to be an error-prone process until I get a sense of these files.

I'm ready to start. I decide to do a quick search of the Web, and I come up with a few patterns for phone numbers. Some of these are a little esoteric, but I'm willing to try them because my client wants as many candidates as possible. The patterns I found are as follows:

^(\(?\+?[0-9]*\)?)?[0-9_\- \(\)]*$

^([0-1]([\s-./\\])?)?(\(?[2-9]\d{2}\)?

[2-9]\d{3})([\s-./\\])?(\d{3}([\s-./\\])?\d{4}

[a-zA-Z0-9]{7})$

^\(?[\d]{3}\)?[\s-]?[\d]{3}[\s-]?[\d]{4}$

I write a quick pattern that ORs these patterns together, run through some documents, and find that, in fact, it doesn't work. Although I'm getting some phone numbers back, I'm also getting some numbers that can't possibly be phone number patterns because they include characters, long spaces, and punctuation.

I have two choices here: I can run a second validation on the candidates that do match, or I can tweak the pattern. This time, I decide to take my own pattern from earlier and try to work in the good traits from the other patterns, as shown in Table 5-5. This is the composition technique introduced in Chapter 1.

Table 5-5. Pulling a General Regex Pattern from 614-345-6789

Step	What I Did	Why I Did It	Justification	Resulting Pattern
Step 1	Nothing	Initial state	N/A	(?:\d{3})?\d{3}\d{4}
Step 2	Put optional - between the number groups	To get a more generic description	The phone number can be delimited with punctuation.	(?:\d{3}-?)?\d{3}-?\d{4}
Step 3	Put optional spaces between the number groups	To get a more generic description	The phone number can be delimited with spaces.	(?:\d{3}-?\s?)?\d{3}-?\s?\d{4}

Table 5-5. Pulling a General Regex Pattern from 614-345-6789 (Continued)

Step	What I Did	Why I Did It	Justification	Resulting Pattern
Step 4	Swapped out - for *\p{Punct}*	To accommodate punctuation	*\p{Punct}* is a superset of -	(?:\d{3}\p{Punct}?\s?)?\d{3}\p{Punct}?\s?\d{4}
Step 5	Replaced *(?:\d{3} \p{Punct}?\s?)? \d{3}\p{Punct}?* with *(?\d{3}\p{Punct }?\s?){1,2}*	To create a more succinct pattern	The two are equivalent statements.	(?:\d{3}\p{Punct}?\s?){1,2}\d{4}

Using this pattern, I find that things seem rational. Finally, just before finishing, I decide to format all of my output in the form *ddd-dddd* or *ddd-ddd-dddd*. The resulting code is shown in Listing 5-12.

Listing 5-12. Extracting Phone Numbers from a File

```
01  /**
02   * mines phone numbers out of the given file, and returns
03   * them as strings.
04   * @param the String filePath of the file
05   * @throws IOException if the file is not found or
06   * is corrupted
07   *
08   * @return ArrayList contained well formatted phone numbers
09   * of the for ddd-ddd-dddd or ddd-dddd
10   */
11  public static ArrayList minePhoneNumbers(String filePath)
12  throws IOException{

13      ArrayList retval = new ArrayList();
14      //get pattern
15      String regex = RegexUtil.getProperty("../regex.properties","allPhones");
```

```
16    //find all the matches
17    Map result =
18       RegexUtil.searchFile(filePath, regex ,Pattern.MULTILINE);

19    //get the matching strings
20    Iterator it = result.values().iterator();

21    //provide a consistent format for phone numbers captured
22    while (it.hasNext())
23    {
24       String num = (String)it.next();
25       num = num.replaceAll("\\p{Punct}|\\s","");

26       if (num.length() == 7)
27         num=num.replaceAll("(\\d{3})(\\d{4})","$1-$2");
28       else
29         num=num.replaceAll("(\\d{3})(\\d{3})(\\d{4})","($1)-$2-$3");

30     retval.add(num);
31    }

32    return retval;
33 }
```

Listing 5-12 is fairly self-explanatory. However, I do want to point out lines 27 and 29. Notice how easy it was to make a minor adjustment and produce well-formatted, consistent output here. Line 27, for example, simply says, "I'd like to capture the first three digits in group number 1 and the last four digits in group number 2. Then, I'd like to separate those two groups with a hyphen." Again, this involved very easy, but ultimately very powerful, code.

Searching a Directory for a File That Contains a Regex Expression

In principle, searching a directory for a file that matches a particular pattern is fairly easy. I already have a mechanism in place to search a file, so all I have to do is search a list of files. As you can see in Figure 5-3, the algorithm is recursive.

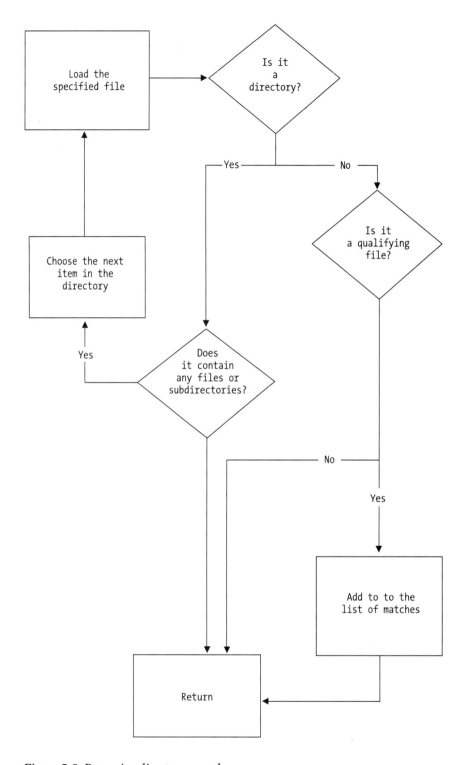

Figure 5-3. Recursive directory search

Listing 5-13 implements this design by taking advantage of the existing frame-works. It searches through subdirectories, looking for files that happen to contain the regex pattern I described.

Listing 5-13. Search Current and Subdirectories for File Containing the Pattern

```
01   /**
02   * Searches through the given directory and finds
03   * the specified files, based the searchPattern that describes
04   * its content. Returns matching files in an ArrayList. This
05   * method searches recursively through the file system.
06   * @param the File currentFile the directory, or file, to start
07   * searching in
08   * @param the String fileExtension, if any, of the file
09   * @param the String searchPattern, the regex that describes
10   * the file content we're looking for
11   * @param the int flags and flags we want to apply to the regex
12   * pattern.
13   * @throws IOException if there's an IO problem
14   *
15   * @return ArrayList containing <code>File</code> objects,
16   * or an empty ArrayList, if no matches are found
17   */
18   public static ArrayList searchDirs(
19       File currentFile,
20       String fileExtension,
21       String searchPattern,
22       int flags
23   ) throws IOException
24   {
25       ArrayList retval = new ArrayList();

26       if (!currentFile.isDirectory())
27       {
28           Map tmp = searchFile(
29               currentFile.getPath(),
30               searchPattern,flags);

31           //if anything was found, add the file
32           if (tmp.size() > 0)
33           {
34               retval.add(currentFile);
35               this.log.finest("added " + currentFile);
36           }
37       }
```

```
38      else
39      {   //step through subdirectories
40          File subs[]  =
41            currentFile.listFiles(
42                newLocalFileFilter(fileExtension));

43          if (subs != null)
44          {
45            //if the recursive search found anything, add it
46            for (int i=0; i < subs.length; i++)
47            {
48                ArrayList tmp=null;
49                tmp =searchDirs(
50                    subs[i],
51                    fileExtension,
52                    searchPattern,
53                    flags);

54                if (tmp.size() > 0)
55                {
56                    log.info(subs[i].getPath());
57                    retval.addAll(tmp);
58                }
59            }
60          }
61      }

62      return retval;
63   }
64 /**
65 * private filtering class, so that file
66 * searches can be more efficient
67 */
68 private static class LocalFileFilter implements FileFilter{
69     private String extension;
70     LocalFileFilter()
71     {
72         this(null);
73     }

74     LocalFileFilter(String extension)
75     {
76         this.extension = extension;
77     }
```

```
78      /**
79       * true if the current file meets the criteria
80       * @param the file pathname to check
81       *
82       * @return true if the file has the extension, or
83       * equals null, or the file is a directory.
84       * Else, returns false.
85       */
86      public boolean accept(File pathname){

87          boolean retval = false;
88          if (extension == null)
89          {
90              retval =  true;
91          }
92          else
93          {
94              String tmp = pathname.getPath();
95              if (tmp.endsWith(extension)) retval =  true;
96              if (pathname.isDirectory()) retval =  true;
97          }

98          return retval;
99      }
100 }
```

Validating an EDI Document

This next example is taken from a posting on the Sun site. A programmer needs help validating an Electronic Data Interchange (EDI) document. He needs to make sure that the String *ISA* always occurs before the String *IEA*, and that each occurs only once. He provided the sample input
ISA*XX*XXXXXXXXXXXXXXX*XX*XXXXXXXXXXXXXXX*030130*0912*~
IEA*1*000005900~.

    This problem is a candidate for the push technique, because it's fairly clear that I'll have to push the data into a pattern. To simplify the problem, I decide to deal in the abstract a bit. Instead of the strings *ISA* and *IEA*, I decide to use the @ sign and the # sign. Furthermore, I decide that everything—all the stuff in between @ and #—is a number. These are just logical placeholders, for my own benefit. I want to be able abstract away some of the messy details.

> **NOTE** If you happened to have liked mathematics in school, you'll notice that this is similar to the algebraic technique of factoring out messy subexpressions and referring to them using a simple variable.

Now I'll see if I can take this anywhere with the reasoning in Table 5-6.

Table 5-6. Pulling a General Regex Pattern from @45#78

Step	What I Did	Why I Did It	Justification	Resulting Pattern
Step 1	Nothing	Initial state	N/A	@45#87
Step 2	Substituted *[^@]* for *4*	To get a more generic description	The only distinguishing feature of *4* is that it's not @, hence *[^@]*.	@[^@]5#7
Step 3	Substituted *[^@]* for *5*	To get a more generic description	The only distinguishing feature of *5* is that it's not @.	@[^@][^@]#7
Step 4	Swapped in *[^@]** for *[^@][^@]*	To get a more generic description	*[^@]** is a superset of *[^@]*.	@[^@]*#7
Step 5	Swapped in *([^@][^#])* for *7*	To get a more generic description	The only distinguishing feature of *7* is that it's not @ or #.	@[^@]*#([^@][^#])8
Step 6	Swapped in *([^@][^#])* for *8*	To get a more generic description	The only distinguishing feature of *8* is that it's not @ or #.	@[^@]*#([^@][^#])([^@][^#])
Step 7	Swapped in *([^@][^#])** for *([^@][^#])([^@][^#])*	To get a more generic description	*([^@][^#])** is a superset of *([^@][^#])([^@][^#])*.	@[^@]*#([^@][^#])*

I think I've taken that about as far as I can. Now I'll start stepping away from the abstract and heading back toward what I actually wanted. Table 5-7 breaks down my reasoning.

Table 5-7. Pulling an EDI Regex out of @[^@]*#([^@][^#])*

Step	What I Did	Why I Did It	Justification	Resulting Pattern
Step 8	Nothing	Initial state	N/A	@[^@]*#([^@][^#])*
Step 9	Substitute *ISA* for @	To get a more specific description	@ was always just a stand-in for *ISA*.	ISA[^ISA]*#([^ISA][^#])*
Step 10	Substitute *IEA* for #	To get a more specific description	# was always just a stand-in for *IEA*.	ISA[^ISA]*IEA([^ISA][^IEA])*
Step 11	Added *?:* inside *([^ISA][^IEA])*	To improve efficiency	I don't need a capturing group.	ISA[^ISA]*IEA(?:[^ISA][^IEA])*

Summary

The examples in this chapter should act as samples for writing your own regex expressions. I discussed confirming zip codes, using date formats, searching a string, searching a file, extracting data from a file, and modifying the contents of a file. If you're looking for more examples like these, please visit http://www.influxs.com.

FAQs

Q: Where can I get more information about a particular pattern?

A: I suggest that you ask the folks at one of the various Java newsgroups. The JavaRanch site (`http://www.javaranch.com`) is particularly helpful, and so are the good folks on the ORO and Regexp newsgroups. Also, Apress now provides forums (`http://forums.apress.com`) where readers can interact directly with authors. When you ask your question, make sure you provide sample input, expected output, and your current code.

Q: What are some other resources for regex?

A: The single best regex book I can think of is Jeffery E. F. Friedl's *Mastering Regular Expressions* (O'Reilly & Associates, 2002). It's an elegant introduction to regex, and it deals with how several languages, including Java, use regex. It doesn't focus on Java regex with the detail that this book does, but it does provide an excellent, entertaining, and detailed account of regex mechanics, theory, and application. If you're looking for a book that will expand your general understanding of regex, you should seriously consider purchasing *Mastering Regular Expressions*.

Q: Can I e-mail you with regex questions?

A: Well, yes and no. I won't address private e-mail messages, but you're likely to find me lurking on the JavaRanch site (`http://www.javaranch.com`) and the Apress forums (`http://forums.apress.com`). If your questions are posted so that the general public can take advantage of the discussion, then I'll try and provide whatever help I can.

APPENDIX A

Regular Expression Reference

THIS APPENDIX PROVIDES a comprehensive quick reference for your day-to-day Java regular expression needs. The material in this appendix is presented as pure regex patterns, not the Java String-delimited counterparts. For example, when referring to a digit, *\d*, not *\\d*, is used here.

Table A-1. Common Characters

Regex	Description	Notes
q	The character *q*	Could be any character, not including special regex characters or punctuation.
\\	The backslash (/) character	\ delimits special regex characters, of which the backslash is a member.
\t	The tab character	
\n	The newline or linefeed character	
\r	The carriage-return character	
\f	The form-feed character	

Table A-2. Predefined Character Classes

Regex	Description	Notes
.	Any single character	Matches any single character, including spaces, punctuation, letters, or numbers. It may or may not match line-termination characters, depending on the operating system involved, or if the DOTALL flag is active in the regex pattern. Thus, it's probably a good idea to explicitly set, or turn off, DOTALL support in your patterns, in case you need to port your code.
\d	Any single digit from 0 to 9	
\D	Will match any character except a single digit	By default, this won't match line terminators.
\s	A whitespace character: *[\t\n\x0B\f\r]*	This matches tab, space, end-of-line, carriage-return, form-feed, and newline characters.
\S	A non-whitespace character	Matches anything that is not a whitespace character, as described previously. Thus, *7* would be matched, as would punctuation.
\w	A word character: *[a-zA-Z_0-9]*	Any uppercase or lowercase letter, digit, or the underscore character.
\W	A nonword character; the opposite of \w	Anything that isn't a word character, as described previously. Thus, the minus sign will match, as will a space. It won't match the end-of-line *$* or beginning-of-line ^ characters.

Table A-3. Character Classes

Regex	Description	Notes
[abc]	*a*, *b*, or *c*	Strictly speaking, it won't match *ab*.
[^abc]	Any character except *a*, *b*, or *c*	This will match any character except *a*, *b*, or *c*. It won't match the end-of-line *$* or beginning-of-line *^* characters.
[a-zA-Z]	Any uppercase or lowercase letter	When working with numbers, *[0-25]* doesn't mean 0 to 25. It means 0 to 2, or just 5. If you wanted 0 to 25, you would need to actually write an expression, such as *\d|1\d|2[0-5]*. Note that *[0-9]* is exactly equal to *\d*.
[a-c[x-z]]	*a* through *c*, or *x* through *z*	For example, *[1-3[7-9]]* matches 1 through 3, or 7 through 9. No other digit will do.
[a-z&&[a,e]]	*a* or *e*	*[a-z&&[a,e,i,o,u]]* matches all lowercase vowels.
[a-z&&[^bc]]	All lowercase letters except for *b* and *c*	For example, all the prime numbers between 1 and 9 would be *[1-9&&[^4689]]*. That is, 1 through 9, excluding 4, 6, 8, and 9.
[a-d&&[^b-c]]	*a* through *d*, but not *b* through *c*	*[1-9&&[^4-6]]* matches 1 through 3, or 7 through 9. Compare this to the union example presented earlier in this table.

Table A-4. POSIX Character Classes

Regex	Description	Notes
\p{Lower}	A lowercase alphabetic character	
\p{Upper}	An uppercase alphabetic character	
\p{ASCII}	An ASCII character	
\p{Alpha}	An alphabetic character	
\p{Digit}	A decimal digit	
\p{Alnum}	An alphanumeric character	
\p{Punct}	Punctuation	This is a good way to deal with punctuation in general, without having to delimit special characters such as periods, parentheses, brackets, and such. It matches *!"#$%&'()*+,-./:;<=>?@[\]^_`{|}~*.
\p{Graph}	A visible character	Exactly equal to *[\p{Alnum}\p{Punct}]*.
\p{Print}	A printable character	Exactly equal to *[\p{Graph}]*.
\p{Blank}	A space or a tab	
\p{Space}	Any whitespace character	It matches *[\t\n\x0B\f\r]*.
\p{Cntrl}	A control character	
\p{XDigit}	A hexadecimal digit	

Table A-5. Boundary Matchers

Regex	Description	Notes
^	Beginning-of-line character	This is an invisible character.
$	End-of-line character	This is an invisible character.
\b	A word boundary	This is the position of a word boundary. Its usage requires some caution, because \b doesn't match characters; it matches a position. Thus, the String *anna marrie* doesn't match the regex *anna\bmarie*. However, it does match *anna\b\smarrie*. That's because there's a word boundary at the position after the last *a* in *anna*, and it happens to be the space character, so \s is necessary to match it, and *marie* must then follow it. Because \b matches a position, it is meaningless to add greedy qualifiers to it. Thus, *\b+*, *\b\b\b\b\b*, and *\b* all match exactly the same thing. Further complicating the picture is the fact that in a character class, \b means a backspace character. This is syntactically legal (if a little awkward) because the word boundary has no place inside a character class. Thus, *[\b]* describes a backspace character, because it is surrounded by *[* and *]*.
\B	A non-word boundary	This is the opposite of word boundary, as described previously.
\A	The beginning of the input	\A matches the beginning of the input, but it isn't just a synonym for the ^ pattern. This distinction becomes clear if you use the `Pattern.MULTILINE` flag when you compile your pattern. \A matches the beginning of the input, which is the very beginning of the file. By contrast, ^ matches the beginning of each line when the `Pattern.MULTILINE` flag is active.
\Z	The end of the input except for the final $, if any	\Z matches the end of the input, but it isn't just a synonym for the $ character. This distinction becomes clear if you use the `Pattern.MULTILINE` flag when you compile your pattern. \Z matches the end of the input, which is the very end of the file. By contrast, $ matches the end of each line when the `Pattern.MULTILINE` flag is active.
\G	The end of the previous match	
\z	The end of the input	This behaves exactly like the \Z with a capital *Z* character, except that it also captures the closing $ character.

Table A-6. Greedy Quantifiers

Regex	Description	Notes
X?	*X*, once or not at all	*A?* would match *A*, or the absence of *A*. This applies to either the character that immediately precedes it, or a group (if the group immediately precedes it), or a character class (if the character class immediately precedes it).
X*	*X*, zero or more times	This pattern is very much like the *?* pattern, except that it matches zero or more occurrences. It doesn't match "any character," as its usage in DOS might indicate. Thus, *A** would match *A*, *AA*, *AAA*, or the absence of *A*. This applies to either the character that immediately precedes it, or a group (if the group immediately precedes it), or a character class (if the character class immediately precedes it).
X+	*X*, one or more times	This quantifier is very much like the *** pattern, except that it looks for the existence of one or more occurrences instead of zero or more occurrences. This applies to either the character that immediately precedes it, or a group (if the group immediately precedes it), or a character class (if the character class immediately precedes it).
X{n}	*X*, exactly *n* times	This quantifier demands the occurrence of the target exactly *n* times. This applies to either the character that immediately precedes it, or a group (if the group immediately precedes it), or a character class (if the character class immediately precedes it).
X{n,}	*X*, at least *n* times	This quantifier demands the occurrence of the target at least *n* times. This applies to either the character that immediately precedes it, or a group (if the group immediately precedes it), or a character class (if the character class immediately precedes it).
X{n,m}	*X*, at least *n* but not more than *m* times	This quantifier demands the occurrence of the target at least *n* times, but not more than *m* times. This applies to either the character that immediately precedes it, or a group (if the group immediately precedes it), or a character class (if the character class immediately precedes it).

Table A-7. Reluctant Quantifiers

Regex	Description	Notes
X??	*X*, once or not at all	This pattern is very much like the *?* pattern, except that it prefers to match nothing at all. When it's used with the Matcher.matches() method, *??* functions in exactly the same way as the *?* pattern. However, when it's used with Matcher.find(), the behavior is different. For example, the pattern *x??*, as applied to the String *xx*, will actually not find *x*, yet consider that lack of finding a success. That's because we asked it to be reluctant to match, and the most reluctant thing it can do is match zero occurrences of *x*. This applies to either the character that immediately precedes it, or a group (if the group immediately precedes it), or a character class (if the character class immediately precedes it).
X*?	*X*, zero or more times	This pattern is very much like the *** pattern, except that it prefers to match as little as possible. When it's used with the Matcher.matches() method, **?* functions in exactly the same way as the *** pattern. However, when it's used with Matcher.find(), the behavior is different. For example, the pattern *x*?*, as applied to the String *xx*, will actually not find *x*, yet consider that a success. That's because we asked it to be reluctant to match, and the most reluctant thing it can do is match zero occurrences of *x*. This applies to either the character that immediately precedes it, or a group (if the group immediately precedes it), or a character class (if character the class immediately precedes it).
X+?	*X*, one or more times	This pattern is very much like the *+* pattern, except that it prefers to match as little as possible. When it's used with the Matcher.matches() method, *+?* functions in exactly the same way as the *+* pattern. However, when it's used with Matcher.find(), the behavior is different. For example, the pattern *x+?*, as applied to the String *xx*, will actually find one *x*, yet consider that a success. That's because we asked it to be reluctant to match, and the most reluctant thing it can do is match one occurrence of *x*. This applies to either the character that immediately precedes it, or a group (if the group immediately precedes it), or a character class (if the character class immediately precedes it).

Table A-7. Reluctant Quantifiers (Continued)

Regex	Description	Notes
X{n}?	*X*, exactly *n* times	This pattern is exactly like the *X{n}* pattern. This applies to either the character that immediately precedes it, or a group (if the group immediately precedes it), or a character class (if the character class immediately precedes it).
X(n,}?	*X*, at least *n* times	This pattern is very much like the *X{n,}* pattern, except that it prefers to match as little as possible. When it's used with the `Matcher.matches()` method, *X{n,}?* functions in exactly the same way as the *X{n,}* pattern. However, when it's used with `Matcher.find()`, the behavior is different. For example, the pattern *X{3,}?*, as applied to the String *xxxxx*, will actually only find *xxx*, yet consider that a success. Compare this with just *X{3,5}*, which would have found *xxxxx*. That's because we asked it to be reluctant to match, and the most reluctant thing it can do is match three occurrences of *x*. This applies to either the character that immediately precedes it, or a group (if the group immediately precedes it), or a character class (if the character class immediately precedes it).
X{n,m}?	*X*, at least *n* but not more than *m* times	This pattern is very much like the *X{n,m}* pattern, except that it prefers to match as little as possible. When it's used with the `Matcher.matches()` method, *X{n,m}?* functions in exactly the same way as the *X{n,m}* pattern. However, when it's used with `Matcher.find()`, the behavior is distinct. For example, the pattern *X{3,5}?*, as applied to the String *xxxxx*, will actually find *xxx*, yet consider that a success. Compare this with just *X{3,5}*, which would have found *xxxxx*. This happens because we asked it to be reluctant to match, and the most reluctant thing it can do is match three occurrences of *x*. Notice that if there were six *x* characters, such as *xxxxxx*, the pattern would have matched twice: once for the first three *xxx* characters and then again for the other three. Again, this is because three is the minimum requirement. This applies to either the character that immediately precedes it, or a group (if the group immediately precedes it), or a character class (if the character class immediately precedes it).

Table A-8. Possessive Quantifiers

Regex	Description	Notes
X?+	*X*, once or not at all	Very much like the *?* pattern, this pattern prefers to match as much as possible. However, this pattern won't release matches to help the entire expression match as a whole. For example, the pattern *w?+**d*, as applied to the String *A2*, will actually not match, because the first *w?+* consumes the *A* and the *2*, and it won't release them for the greater good of allowing the entire expression to match. Thus, *d* is unable to match. This is because we asked *w?+* to be possessive, and the most possessive thing it can do is match the occurrence of *A* and *2*, and not release them. This applies to either the character that immediately precedes it, or a group (if the group immediately precedes it), or a character class (if the character class immediately precedes it).
X*+	*X*, zero or more times	Very much like the *** pattern, this pattern prefers to match as much as possible. However, this pattern won't release matching to help the entire expression as a whole match. For example, the pattern *w*+**d*, as applied to the String *Java2*, will actually not match, because the first *w*+* consumes the String *Java2* and won't release it for the greater good of allowing the entire expression to match. Thus, *d* is unable to match. This is because the pattern *w*+* is possessive, and the most possessive thing it can do is match the entire *Java2* and not release anything. This applies to either the character that immediately precedes it, or a group (if the group immediately precedes it), or a character class (if the character class immediately precedes it).

Table A-8. Possessive Quantifiers (Continued)

Regex	Description	Notes
X++	*X*, one or more times	Very much like the + pattern, this pattern prefers to match as much as possible. However, this pattern won't release matching to help the entire expression as a whole match. For example, the pattern \w++\d, as applied to the String *Java2*, will actually not match, because the first \w++ consumes the String *Java2* and won't release it for the greater good of allowing the entire expression to match. Thus, \d is unable to match. This is because the pattern \w++ is possessive, and the most possessive thing it can do is match the entire *Java2* and not release anything. This applies to either the character that immediately precedes it, or a group (if the group immediately precedes it), or a character class (if the character class immediately precedes it).
X{n}+	*X*, exactly *n* times	This pattern is exactly like the *X{n}* pattern. This applies to either the character that immediately precedes it, or a group (if the group immediately precedes it), or a character class (if the character class immediately precedes it).
X(n,}+	*X*, at least *n* times	Very much like the *X{n,}* pattern, this pattern prefers to match as much as possible. However, this pattern won't release matching to help the entire expression as a whole match. For example, the pattern \w{4,}+\d, as applied to the String *Java2*, will actually not match, because the \w{4,}+ consumes the String *Java2* and won't release it for the greater good of allowing the entire expression to match. Thus, \d is unable to match *4*. This is because the pattern \w{4,}+ is possessive, and the most possessive thing it can do is match the entire *Java2* and not release anything. This pattern applies to either the character that immediately precedes it, or a group (if the group immediately precedes it), or a character class (if the character class immediately precedes it).

Table A-8. Possessive Quantifiers (Continued)

Regex	Description	Notes
X{n,m}+	*X*, at least *n* but not more than *m* times	Very much like the *X{n,m}* pattern, this pattern prefers to match as much as possible. However, this pattern won't release matching to help the entire expression as a whole match. For example, the pattern *\x{2,5}\d*, as applied to the String *Java2*, will actually not match, because the first *\w++* consumes the String *Java2*, and won't release it for the greater good of allowing the entire expression to match. Thus, *\d* is unable to match. This is because the pattern *\x{2,5}* is possessive, and the most possessive thing it can do is match the entire *Java2* and not release anything. This applies to either the character that immediately precedes it, or a group (if the group immediately precedes it), or a character class (if the character class immediately precedes it).

Table A-9. Logical Operators

Regex	Description	Notes
XY	*X* followed by *Y*	This is the default relationship assumption between characters. Note that spaces are a valid part of this syntax. Thus, *A B* means the character *A*, followed by a space, followed by the character *B*.
X|Y	Either *X* or *Y*	*AB|CD* will match either *AB* or *CD*. Similarly, the pattern *hello sir|madam* will match *hello sir* or it will match *madam*. Specifically, it won't match *hello madam*. This is because of the nature of the And pattern discussed previously. When the regex engine sees *hello sir*, it assumes you mean that *hello*, followed by a space, followed by *sir* should be treated as a single logical unit. These are all Anded together. Then the engine sees the Or pattern, so it assumes that the logical alternative is *madam*. If you actually want to accept *hello sir* or *hello madam*, you'll have to use groups—thus, the pattern *hello (sir|madam)*. Or better yet, you can use the noncapturing group *hello (?:sir|madam)*.

Table A-9. Logical Operators (Continued)

Regex	Description	Notes
(X)	*X*, the capturing group	A capturing group is a logical unit that is conceptually similar to the logical units you're familiar with from algebra. Thus, *(\d\d\d\d)* is a capturing group that defines four digits. Capturing groups can be referred to later in your expression by using a back reference, as explained later. They're counted left to right and can be nested. Thus, *h(ello (world))* has three capturing groups. Capturing group 0 is the entire expression, which matches the String *hello world*. Capturing group 1 is *ello world*, because you count from left to right, and the first group starts with the *(* right before the *e* in *hello*. Group 2 is *world*, because the second group starts right before the *w* in *world*.
\n	The *n*th capturing group matched	In this context, I'm not referring to newline, even though \n looks like the newline symbol. The *n* in this case refers to a number. The regex engine allows you to access the information captured by a previous part of the group, even as the search is executing. For example, if you want to find repeated words, all you need is the pattern *(\w+)\W\1*, which says, "Look for a group of word characters, followed by a nonword character, followed by that exact same word character captured in group 1." If you attempt to refer to a group that doesn't exist, a PatternSyntaxException will be thrown. If you happen to have, say, 13 captured groups, then *\13* will mean that you want the thirteenth capturing group. If you don't have 13 groups, then the same expression *\13* will mean the first capturing group, followed by the digit *3*.

Table A-10. Quotation

Regex	Description	Notes
\	Quotes the following character	This quotes the metacharacter that follows, so it will actually be treated as a character. Thus, if you were looking for a dollar sign, you would use *\$.* as the pattern. By contrast, *$* would have matched the end-of-line character. Remember that for regex expressions used directly as Strings, you need to double the number of \ characters you see. Thus, in a Java String, *\s* becomes *\\s*.
\Q	Quotes all characters until *\E*	This works in conjunction with *\E* to quote a sequence of characters. If you need to quote a lot of characters in sequence, then use *\Q* to open your quote and *\E* to close it. For example, if you want the characters *\([?**, the expression *\Q\(?*\E* will do the job.
\E	Ends quote started by *\Q*	

Table A-11. Noncapturing Group Constructs

Regex	Description	Notes
(?:X)	Defines a subpattern as a logical unit	Noncapturing groups don't store the information that actually matches the pattern for later access. These are much more efficient than capturing groups if you're only using grouping for logical purposes. This pattern is noncapturing.
(?idmsux-idmsux)	*i* for CASE_INSENSITIVE *x* for COMMENTS *s* for DOTALL *u* for UNICODE_CASE *m* for MULTILINE *d* for UNIX_LINES	The pattern *(?i)hel(?-i)LO* will match the String *HELLO*, because *(?i)* indicates a case-insensitive match starting from *h*, and *(?-i)* signals an end to that case insensitivity after the first *l*. This pattern is noncapturing.
(?idmsux-idmsux:X)	*X*, with the given flags on or off	The pattern *(?i:hel)LO* will match the String *HELLO*, because *(?i:* indicates a case-insensitive match starting from *h* and ending with the first *l*. This pattern is noncapturing.

Table A-12. Lookarounds

Regex	Description	Notes
(?=X)	*X*, using zero-width positive lookahead	This pattern glances to the right of whatever remains to be parsed from the candidate String to find the first position at which the expression *X* exists. For example, if you want to extract all of the inline comments from a text file, you might try the pattern *(?=//).*$* and extract group 0. This pattern is noncapturing.
(?!X)	*X*, using zero-width negative lookahead	This pattern glances to the right, to whatever remains to be parsed from the candidate String, to find the first position at which the expression *X* doesn't exist. For example, if you want to skip leading spaces leading up to some content, you could use *(?!\s).**. This pattern is noncapturing.
(?<=X)	*X*, using zero-width positive lookbehind	This pattern glances to the left, to whatever remains to be parsed from the candidate String, to find the first position at which the expression *X* exists. For example, if you want to extract all of the inline comments from a text file, you might try the pattern *(?=//).*$*. This pattern is noncapturing.
(?<!X)	*X*, using zero-width negative lookbehind	This pattern glances to the left, to whatever remains to be parsed from the candidate String, to find the first position at which the expression *X* doesn't occur. For example, if you want to extract all of the text before inline Java comments from a text file, you might try the pattern *.*(?<=//)*. This pattern is noncapturing.
(?>X)	*X*, as an independent, non-capturing group	This pattern refuses to release the contents of the match, regardless of the consequences on the rest of the pattern's ability to match. Thus, whereas the pattern *\w+\d* matches the String *java2*, the pattern *(?>\w+)\d* does not, because the *(?>\w+)* consumes *java* and *2*, and refuses to release the *2* so that *\d* can match.

Table A-13. Less Common Characters

Regex	Description	Notes
\0n	The character with octal value *on*	0 <= n <= 7
\0nn	The character with octal value *onn*	0 <= n <= 7
\0mnn	The character with octal value *0mnn*	0 <= m <= 3, 0 <= n <= 7 (This can't exceed 377.)
\xhh	The character with hexadecimal value *0xhh*	0 <= h <= 9 or A<=h <=F
\uhhhh	The character with hexadecimal value *0xhhhh*	0 <= h <= 9 or A<=h <=F
\a	The alert (bell) character ('\u0007')	
\e	The escape character ('\u001B')	
\cx	The control character corresponding to *x*	

Table A-14. Unicode Blocks and Categories

Regex	Description	Notes
\p{InGreek}	A character in the Greek block	
\p{Lu}	An uppercase letter	*\p{Lu}* matches any uppercase character.
\p{Sc}	A currency symbol	If you need to find or swap out, say, a dollar sign, this is a good way to do so without having to deal with the various delimiting complexities of not matching the end-of-line character *$*.
\P{InGreek}	Any character except one in the Greek block (negation)	Notice the use of the capital *P* here. In general, uppercase *\P* is the opposite of lowercase *\p*. Thus, *\P{Lower}* matches all uppercase characters.
[\p{L}&&[^\p{Lu}]]	Any non-uppercase letter	This is exactly equal to *\p{Upper}*.

Pattern and Matcher Methods

THIS APPENDIX PROVIDES a summary of the methods of the `Pattern` and `Matcher` classes in Java. It's intended to be a quick reference for working with the various regex utilities you'll be using. For more detailed descriptions, please see the appropriate section in the text.

Pattern Class Fields

UNIX_LINES

The `UNIX_LINES` flag is used in constructing the second parameter of the `Pattern.compile(String regex, int flags)` method. Use this flag when parsing data that originates on a UNIX machine.

On many flavors of UNIX, the invisible character \n is used to note termination of a line. This is distinct from other operating systems, including flavors of Windows, which may use \r\n, \n,\r, \u2028, or \u0085 for a line terminator.

If you've ever transported a file that originated on a UNIX machine to a Windows platform and opened it, you may have noticed that the lines sometimes don't terminate as you might expect, depending on which editor you use to view the text. This happens because the two systems can use different syntax to denote the end of the line.

The `UNIX_LINES` flag simply tells the regex engine that it's dealing with UNIX style lines, which affects the matching behavior of the regular expression metacharacters ^ and $.

> **NOTE**   Using the `UNIX_LINES` flag, or the equivalent *(?d)* regex pattern, doesn't degrade performance. By default, this flag isn't set.

CASE_INSENSITIVE

The CASE_INSENSITIVE field is used in constructing the second parameter of the Pattern.compile(String regex, int flags) method. It's useful when you need to match U.S. ASCII characters, regardless of case.

> **NOTE** Using this flag, or the equivalent *(?i)* regular expression, can cause performance to degrade slightly. By default, this flag is not set.

COMMENTS

The COMMENTS field is defined because it's used in constructing the second parameter of the Pattern.compile(String regex, int flags) method. It tells the regex engine that the regex pattern has an embedded comment in it. Specially, it tells the regex engine to ignore any comments in the pattern, starting with the spaces leading up to the # character and everything thereafter, until the end of the line.

Thus, the regex pattern *A   #matches uppercase US-ASCII char code 65* will use *A* as the regular expression, but the spaces leading up to the # character and everything thereafter until the end of the line will be ignored.

> **NOTE** Using this flag, or the equivalent *(?x)* regular expression, doesn't degrade performance.

MULTILINE

The MULTILINE field is used in constructing the second parameter of the Pattern.compile(String regex, int flags) method. It tells the regex engine that regex input isn't a single line of code; rather, it contains several lines that have their own termination characters.

This means that the beginning-of-line character, *^*, and the end-of-line character, *$*, will potentially match several lines within the input String.

For example, imagine that your input String is *This is sentence.\n So is this.* If you use the MULTILINE flag to compile the regular expression pattern:

```
Pattern p = Pattern.compile("^", Pattern.MULTILINE);
```

then the beginning of line character, ^, will match before the *T* in *This is a sentence.* It will also match just before the *S* in *So is this.* Without using the MULTILINE flag, the match will only find the *T* in *This is a sentence.*

> **NOTE** Using this flag, or the equivalent *(?m)* regular expression, may degrade performance.

DOTALL

The DOTALL flag is used in constructing the second parameter of the Pattern.compile(String regex, int flags) method.

The DOTALL flag tells the regex engine to allow the metacharacter period (.) to match any character, *including* a line termination character. What does this mean?

Imagine that your candidate String were *Test\n.* If your corresponding regex pattern were the period (.), then you would normally have four matches: one for the *T*, another for the *e*, another for *s*, and the fourth for *t*. This is because the regex metacharacter period (.) will normally match any character, except line termination characters.

Enabling the DOTALL flag

```
Pattern p = Pattern.compile(".", Pattern.DOTALL);
```

would have generated five matches. Your pattern would have matched the *T*, *e*, *s*, and *t* characters. In addition, it would have matched the \n character at the end of the line.

> **NOTE** Using this flag, or the equivalent *(?s)* regular expression, doesn't degrade performance.

UNICODE_CASE

The UNICODE_CASE flag in conjunction with the CASE_INSENSITIVE flag generates case-insensitive matches for international character sets.

> **NOTE** Using this flag, or the equivalent *(?u)* regular expression, can degrade performance.

CANON_EQ

As you know, characters are actually stored as numbers. For example, in the U.S. ASCII character set, the character A is represented by the number 65. Depending on the character set that you're using, the same character can be represented by different numeric combinations. For example, *à* can be represented by both +00E0 and U+0061U+0300. A CANON_EQ match would match either representation.

> **NOTE** Using this flag may degrade performance.

Pattern Class Methods

public static Pattern compile(String regex) throws PatternSyntaxException

You'll notice that the Pattern class doesn't have a public constructor. This means that you can't write the following type of code:

```
Pattern p = new Pattern("my regex");//wrong!
```

To get a reference to a Pattern object, you must use the static method pattern(String regex). Thus, your first line of regex code might look like the following:

```
Pattern p = Pattern.compile("my regex");//Right!
```

The parameter for this method is a String that represents a regular expression. When passing a String to a method that expects a regular expression, it's important to delimit any \ characters that the regular expressions might have by appending another \ character to them. This is because String objects internally use the \ character to delimit metacharacters in a character sequences, regardless of whether those character sequences are regular expressions. This has been true long before regular expression were a part of Java. Thus, the regular expression *d* becomes *d*. To match a single digit, your regular expression code becomes the following:

```
Pattern p = Pattern.compile("\\d");
```

The point here is that the regular expression *d* becomes the String *d*.

The delimitation of the String parameter can sometimes be tricky, so it's important to understand it well. By and large, it means that you double the \ characters that might already be present in the regular expression. It doesn't mean that you simply append a single \ character.

The compile method will throw a java.util.regex.PatternSyntaxException if the regular expression itself is badly formed. For example, if you pass in a String that contains *[4*, the compile method will throw a PatternSyntaxException at runtime, because the syntax of the regular expression *[4* is illegal.

The compile(String regex) method returns a Pattern object.

public static compile pattern(String regex, int flags) throws PatternSyntaxException

The compile(String regex, int flags) method is a more powerful form of the compile method. The first parameter for this method, regex, is a String that represents a regular expression, as detailed in the previous pattern.compile(String regex) method entry. For details on how the String parameter must be formatted, please see the previous compile(String regex) method entry.

The flexibility of this compile method is fully realized by using the second parameter, int flags. For example, if you want a match to be successful regardless of the case of the candidate String, then your pattern might look like the following:

```
Pattern p = Pattern.compile(regex,Pattern.CASE_INSENSITIVE);
```

You can combine the flags by using the | operator. For example, to achieve case-insensitive Unicode matches that include a comment, you might use the following:

```
Pattern p =
Pattern.compile("t # a compound flag example",Pattern.CASE_INSENSITIVE |
        Pattern.UNICODE_CASE| Pattern.COMMENT);
```

The `compile(String regex, int flags)` method returns a `Pattern` object.

public String pattern()

This method returns the regular expression from which this pattern was compiled. This is a simple `String` that represents the regex you passed in.

This method can be misleading in two ways. First, the `String` that is returned doesn't reflect any flags that were set when the pattern was compiled. Second, the regex `String` you passed in isn't always the pattern `String` you get back out. Specifically, the original `String` delimitations aren't shown. Thus, if your original code was

```
Pattern p = Pattern.compile("\\d");
```

then you should expect your output to be \d, with a single \ character.

public Matcher matcher(CharSequence input)

Remember that you create a `Pattern` object by compiling a description of what you're looking for. A `Pattern` lists the features of what you're looking for. Speaking purely conceptually, your patterns might look like the following:

```
Pattern p = Pattern.compile("She must have red hair and be smarter than I am");
```

Correspondingly, you'll need to compare that description against candidates. That is, you'll want to examine a given `String` to see whether it matches the description you provided.

The `Matcher` object is designed specifically to help you do this sort of interrogation. The `Pattern.matcher(CharSequence input)` method returns the `Matcher` that will help get details about how your candidate `String` compares with the description you passed in.

public int flags()

Earlier, I discussed the constant flags that you can use in compiling your regex pattern. The flags method simply returns an `int` that represents those flags.

To see if your `Pattern` class is currently using a given flag—for example, the `Pattern.COMMENTS` flag—simply extract the flag

```
int flgs  = myPattern.flags();
```

and then & that flag to the `Pattern.COMMENTS` flag:

```
boolean isUsingCommentFlag =(  Pattern.COMMENTS == (Pattern.COMMENTS & flgs)) ;
```

Similarly, to see if you're using `CASE_insensitive`, do the following:

```
boolean isUsingCaseInsensitiveFlag =
(Pattern.CASE_insensitive == (Pattern. CASE_insensitive & flgs));
```

public static boolean matches(String regex,CharSequence input)

Very often, you'll find that all you need to know about a `String` is whether it matches a given regular expression exactly. You don't want to have to create a `Pattern` object, extract its `Matcher` object, and interrogate that `Matcher`.

This static utility method is designed to help you do exactly that. Internally, it creates the `Pattern` and `Matcher` objects you need, compares the regex to the input `String`, and returns a Boolean indicating whether the two objects match exactly. Usage might look something like `PatternMatchesTest` example shown here:

```
import java.util.regex.*;
public class PatternMatchesTest{
  public static void main(String args[]){

      String regex = "ad*";
      String input = "add";

      boolean isMatch = Pattern.matches(regex,input);
      System.out.println(isMatch);\\return true
  }
}
```

If you're going to be doing a lot of comparisons, then it's more efficient to explicitly create a `Pattern` object and do your matches manually. However, if you're not going to be doing a lot of comparisons, then `matches` is a handy utility method.

The `Pattern.matches(String regex, CharSequence input)` method is also used internally by the `String` class. As of J2SE 1.4, `String` has a new method called `matches`, which internally defers to this one. Thus, you might already be using this method without being aware of it.

Of course, this method can throw a `PatternSyntaxException` if the regex pattern under consideration isn't well formed.

public String[] split(CharSequence input)

This method can be particularly helpful if you need to break up a `String` into an array of substrings based on some criteria. In concept, it's similar to the `StringTokenizer`. However, it's much more powerful and more resource intensive than `StringTokenizer`, because it allows your program to use a regular expressions as the splitting criteria.

This method always returns at least one element. If the split candidate, `input`, can't be found, a `String` array is returned that contains exactly one `String`, namely the original `input`.

If the `input` can be found, then a `String` array is returned. That array contains every substring after an occurrence of the `input`. Thus, for the pattern

```
Pattern p = new Pattern.compile(",");
```

the split method for *Hello, Dolly* will return a `String` array consisting of two elements. The first element of the array will contain the `String` *Hello*, and the second will contain the `String` *Dolly*. That `String` array is obtained as follows:

```
String tmp[] = p.split("Hello,Dolly");
```

In this case, the value return is

```
//tmp =={ "Hello", "Dolly"}
```

There are some subtleties you should be aware of when working with this method. If the candidate `String` had been *Hello,Dolly*, with a trailing comma character after the *y* in *Dolly*, then this method would still have returned two elements: a `String` array consisting of *Hello* and *Dolly*. The implicit behavior is that training spaces aren't returned.

If the input `String` had been *Hello,,,Dolly*, the resulting `String` array would have four elements. The return value of the split method, as applied to the `Pattern`, is

```
// p.split("Hello,,,Dolly") == {"Hello","","","Dolly"}
```

The String method further optimizes its search criteria by placing an invisible ^ before the pattern and a $ after it.

public String[] split(CharSequence input, int limit)

This method works in exactly the same way as Pattern.split(CharSequence input), with one variation. The second parameter, limit, allows you to control how many elements are returned:

Limit == 0

If you specify that the second parameter, limit, should equal 0, then this method behaves exactly like its overloaded counterpart:

Limit >0

Use a positive limit if you're interested in only a certain number of matches. You should use number *1* as the limit. Say the Pattern **p** has been compiled for the String , as previously. To split the String *Hello, Dolly, You, Are, My, Favorite* when you only want the first two tokens, you would use this:

```
String[] tmp = pattern.split("Hello, Dolly, You, Are, My, Favorite",3);
```

The value of the resulting String would be this:

```
//tmp[0] =  "Hello",  tmp[1] = "Dolly";
```

The interesting behavior here is that a third element is returned, in this case

```
//tmp[2] =  "You, Are, My, Favorite";
```

Using a positive limit can potentially lead to performance enhancements, because the regex engine can stop searching when it meets the specified number of matches:

Limit <0

Using a negative number—any negative number—for the limit tells the regex engine that you want to return as many matches as possible *and* that you want trailing spaces, if any, to be returned. Thus, for the regex pattern , and the candidate String *Hello,Dolly* the command

```
String tmp[] = p.split("Hello,Dolly", -1);
```

results in

```
//tmp == {"Hello","Dolly"};
```

However, for the String *Hello, Dolly,<space><space><space>*, with trailing spaces after the comma following the *Dolly*, the method call

```
String tmp[] = p.split("Hello,Dolly,   ", -1);
```

results in

```
//tmp == {"Hello","Dolly","   "};
```

Notice that the actual value of the negative limit doesn't matter. Thus,

```
p.split("Hello,Dolly", -1);
```

is exactly equivalent to

```
p.split("Hello,Dolly", -100);
```

Method Class Methods

public Pattern pattern()

The pattern method returns the Pattern that created this particular Matcher object. The Pattern returned doesn't contain any of the flags that are explicitly set by using the Pattern constants when the pattern is compiled, such as Pattern.MULTILINE.

public Matcher reset()

The reset() method clears all state information from the Matcher object it is called on. The Matcher is, in effect, reverted to the state it originally had when you first received a reference to it.

public Matcher reset(CharSequence input)

The reset(CharSequnce input) method clears the state of the Matcher object it's called on and replaces the candidate String with the new input. This has the same effect as creating a new Matcher object, except that it doesn't have the associated overhead. This recycling can be a useful optimization, and it's one that I often use.

public int start()

This method returns the index of the first character of the candidate String matched. If there are no matches, or if no matches have been attempted, an IllegalStateException is thrown.

public int start(int group)

This method allows you to specify which subgroup within a matching you're interested in and returns the index of the first character in which that subgroup starts. If there are no matches, or if no matches have been attempted, an IllegalStateException is thrown. If you refer to a group number that doesn't exist, an IndexOutOfBoundsException is thrown.

public int end()

The end method returns the ending index plus 1 of the last successful match the Matcher object had. If no matches exist, or if no matches have been attempted, this method throws an IllegalStateException.

public int end(int group)

Like the start(int) method, this method allows you to specify which subgroup within a matching you're interested in, except that it returns the last index of matching character sequence plus 1. If no matches exist, or if no matches have been attempted, this method throws an IllegalStateException. If you refer to a group number that doesn't exist, an IndexOutOfBoundsException is thrown.

public String group()

The group method can be a powerful and convenient tool in the war against jumbled code. It simply returns the substring of the candidate String that matches the original regex pattern. The group() method throws an IllegalStateException if the find method call wasn't successful. Similarly, it throws an IllegalStateException if find has never been called at all.

public String group(int group)

This method is a more powerful counterpart to the group() method. It allows you to extract parts of a candidate string that match a subgroup within your pattern.

The group(int) method throws an IllegalStateException if the find method call wasn't successful. Similarly, it throws an IllegalStateException is find has never been called at all. If called for a group number that doesn't exist, it throws an IndexOutOfBoundsException.

public int groupCount()

This method simply returns the number of groups that the Pattern defined. There's a very important, and somewhat counterintuitive, subtlety to notice about this method: It returns the number of possible groups based on the original Pattern, without even considering the candidate String. Thus, it's not really information about the Matcher object; instead, it's about the Pattern that helped spawn it. This can be tricky, because the fact that this method lives on the Matcher object could be interpreted as meaning that it's providing feedback about the state of the Matcher. It isn't. It's telling you how many matches are theoretically possible for the given Pattern.

public boolean matches()

This method is designed to help you match a candidate String against the matcher's Pattern. It returns true if, and only if, the candidate String under consideration matches the pattern exactly.

public boolean find()

The find() method parses just enough of the candidate String to find a match. If such a substring is found, then true is returned and find stops parsing the candidate. If no part of the candidate String matches the pattern, then find returns false.

public boolean find(int start)

find(int start) works exactly like its overloaded counterpart, with the exception of where it starts searching. The int parameter start simply tells the Matcher at which character to start its search.

Thus, for the candidate String *I love Java. Java is my favorite language. Java Java Java.* and the Pattern **Java**, if you only want to start searching at character index 11, you use the command find(11).

public Matcher appendReplacement(StringBuffer sb, String replacement)

The appendReplace method allows you to modify the contents of a StringBuffer based on a regular expression. It even allows you to use back references by using the *$n* notation, in which *n* refers to some captured subgroup. For example, for the StringBuffer *Waldo Smith*, the Pattern *(\w+) (\w+)*, and the replacement *$2, $1*, the contents of the StringBuffer will be modified to *Smith, Waldo.*

The appendReplacement method will throw an IllegalStateException if a find() hasn't been called, or if find would have returned false if called. It will throw an IndexOutOfBoundsException if the capturing group referred to by *$1, $2*, etc., doesn't exist in the part of the pattern currently being scrutinized by the Matcher.

public StringBuffer appendTail(StringBuffer sb)

The appendTail method is a supplement to the appendReplacement method. It simply appends every remaining subsequence from the original candidate String to the StringBuffer, if reading from the append position, which I explained in the appendReplacement section, to the end of the candidate string.

public String replaceAll(String replacement)

The replaceAll method returns a String that replaces every occurrence of the description with the replacement. Using this method will change the state of your Matcher object. Specifically, the reset() method will be called. Therefore, remember that all start, end, group, and find calls will have to be reexecuted.

Like the appendReplacement method, the replaceAll method can contain references to substring by using the *$* symbol. For details, please see the appendReplacement documentation presented earlier.

public String replaceFirst(String replacement)

The replaceFirst method is a more limited version of the replaceAll method. This method returns a String that replaces the first occurrence of the description with the replacement. Using this method will change the state of your Matcher object. Specifically, the reset() method will be called. Therefore, remember that all start, end, group, and find calls will have to be reexecuted after replaceFirst is called.

Like the appendReplacement method, the replaceFirst method can contain references to substring by using the *$* symbol. For details, please see the appendReplacement documentation presented earlier.

Common Regex Patterns

THIS APPENDIX PRESENTS some practical regex patterns that you can use for common matching and validation tasks.

Table C-1. IP Address ^(([0-1]?\d{1,2}\.)|(2[0-4]\d\.)|(25[0-5]\.)){3} (([0-1]?\d{1,2})|(2[0-4]\d)|(25[0-5]))$

Regex	Description
^	Beginning of line
(	A group consisting of
(	A subgroup consisting of
[0-1]?	Zero or one, both optional, followed by
\d	Any digit
{1,2}	Repeated one or two times, followed by
\.	A period
)	Close subgroup
|	Or
(	A subgroup consisting of
2	The digit 2, followed by
[0-4]	Any digit from 0 to 4, followed by
\d	Any digit, followed by
\.	A period
)	Close subgroup
|	Or
(	A subgroup consisting of
2	The digit 2, followed by
5	The digit 5, followed by

*Table C-1. IP Address ^((([0-1]?\d{1,2}\.)|(2[0-4]\d\.)|(25[0-5]\.)){3}
((([0-1]?\d{1,2})|(2[0-4]\d)|(25[0-5]))$ (Continued)*

Regex	Description
[0-5]	Any digit from *0* to *5*, followed by
\.	A period
)	Close subgroup
)	Close group
{3}	Repeated three times, followed by
(	A group consisting of
(	A subgroup consisting of
[0-1]?	Zero or one, both optional, followed by
\d{1,2}	Any two digits
)	Close subgroup
|	Or
(	A subgroup consisting of
2	The digit *2*, followed by
[0-4]	Any digit from *0* to *4*, followed by
\d	Any digit
)	Close subgroup
|	Or
(	A subgroup consisting of
2	The digit *2*, followed by
5	The digit *5*, followed by
[0-5]	Any digit from *0* to *5*, followed by
)	Close subgroup
)	Subgroup
$	End of line

* **In English:** Three sets of three digits separated by periods, each ranging from 0 to 255, followed by three digits, each ranging from 0 to 255.

> **NOTE** The following pattern also matches the IP address, but all the groups have been marked as noncapturing:
>
> (?:(?:[0-1]?\d{1,2}\.)|(?:2[0-4]\d\.)|(?:25[0-5]\.)){3}(?:(?:[0-1]?\d{1,2})|(?:2[0-4]\d)|(?:25[0-5]))
>
> This is slightly more efficient than the previous pattern, but it's less legible.

Table C-2. Simple E-mail ^(\p{Alnum}+(\.|_|\-)?)*\p{Alnum}@(\p{Alnum}+(\.|_|\-)?)*\p{Alpha}$

Regex	Description
^	Beginning of line
(	A group consisting of
\p{Alnum}	A letter or a digit
+	Repeated one or more times, followed by
(	A subgroup consisting of
\.	A period
|	Or
_	An underscore
|	Or
\-	A hyphen
)	Close subgroup
?	The preceding punctuation is optional
)	Close group
*	The previous group can be repeated zero or more times, followed by
\p{Alnum}	A letter or a digit, followed by
@	An @ symbol, followed by
\p{Alnum}	A letter or a digit
+	Repeated one or more times, followed by

Table C-2. Simple E-mail ^(\p{Alnum}+(\.|_|\-)?)*\p{Alnum}@(\p{Alnum}+ (\.|_|\-)?)*\p{Alpha}$ (Continued)

Regex	Description
(	A group consisting of
\.	A period
|	Or
_	An underscore
|	Or
\-	A hyphen
)	Close group
?	The preceding punctuation is optional
\p{Alpha}	An upper- or lowercase letter
$	End of line

* **In English:** Any number of alphanumeric characters followed by single hyphens, periods, or underscores, but ending in an alphanumeric character; followed by an @ symbol; followed by any number of alphanumeric characters; followed by single hyphens, periods, or underscores, but ending in an upper- or lowercase character.

NOTE The following pattern matches the previous one exactly, except that it allows an IP address as well:

^(\p{Alnum}+(\.|_|\-)?)*\p{Alnum}@(((\p{Alnum}+(\.|_|\-)?)* \p{Alpha})|((([0-1]?\d{1,2}\.)|(2[0-4]\d\.)|(25[0-5]\.)){3}(([0-1]?\d{1,2})| (2[0-4]\d)|(25[0-5]))))$

For a breakdown of the IP address pattern, please see Table C-1.

Table C-3. Digit Repeated Exactly n Times \d{n}, Where n Is the Number of Digits Needed

Regex	Description
\d	Any number
{n}	Repeated *n* times

* **In English:** *n* digits. Thus, if *n* was equal to 4, any four digits.

Table C-4. Characters Repeated Exactly n Times \w{n}, Where n Is the Number of Characters Needed

Regex	Description
\w	Any number, any digit, or an underscore symbol
{n}	Repeated *n* times

* **In English:** *n* characters. Thus, if *n* was equal to 4, any four characters.

Table C-5. Characters Repeated n to m Times \w{n.m}, Where n Is the Number of Characters Needed

Regex	Description
\w	Any number, any digit, or an underscore symbol
{n	Repeated *n* times
m}	But not more than *m* times

* **In English:** *n* characters. Thus, if *n* was equal to 4 and *m* was equal to 9, any four, five, six, seven, eight, or nine characters.

Table C-6. Credit Cards: Visa, MasterCard, American Express, and Discover
^((4\d{3})|(5[1-5]\d{2})|(6011))-?\d{4}-?\d{4}-?\d{4}|3[4,7]\d{13}$

Regex	Description
^	Beginning of line
(	A group consisting of
(	A subgroup consisting of
4	the digit four, followed by
\d[3]	Any three digits
)	Close subgroup
|	Or
(	A subgroup consisting of
5	The digit *5*, followed by
[1-5]	Any digit ranging from *1* to *5*, followed by
\d[2]	Any two digits
)	Close subgroup
|	Or
(	A subgroup consisting of
6001	The digits *6, 0, 0, 1*
)	Close subgroup, followed by
-?	An optional hyphen, followed by
\d{4]	Any four digits, followed by
-?	An optional hyphen, followed by
\d{4]	Any four digits, followed by
-?	An optional hyphen, followed by
\d{4]	Any four digits, followed by
-?	An optional hyphen
|	Or
3	The digit *3*, followed by

Table C-6. Credit Cards: Visa, MasterCard, American Express, and Discover
^((4\d{3})|(5[1-5]\d{2})|(6011))-?\d{4}-?\d{4}-?\d{4}|3[4,7]\d{13}$ (Continued)

Regex	Description
[4,7]	A *4* or a *7*, followed by
\d{13}	Any thirteen digits, followed by
$	End of line

* **In English:** A number starting with *4* and three digits, or *5* and three digits, or *6011*, followed by a hyphen, followed by three sets of four digits, or 34 and thirteen digits, or 37 and thirteen digits.

> **NOTE** This regex does not, and cannot, conform to mod 10 verification. To find a Java program that does, please visit http://www.influxs.com.

Table C-7. Real Number ^[+-]?\d+(\.\d+)?$

Regex	Description
^	Beginning of line, followed by
[+-]?	An optional plus or a minus sign
\d+	Followed by one or more digits, followed by
(	A group consisting of
\.	A period, followed by
\d+	One or more digits
)?	Close group, and make it optional
$	End of line

* **In English:** Any number of digits followed by an optional decimal component.

Index

ASPToday is a unique solutions library for professional ASP Developers, giving quick and convenient access to a constantly growing library of **over 1000 practical and relevant articles and case studies**. We aim to publish a completely original professionally written and reviewed article every working day of the year. Consequently our resource is completely without parallel in the industry. Thousands of web developers use and recommend this site for real solutions, keeping up to date with new technologies, or simply increasing their knowledge.

Exciting Site Features!

Find it FAST!
Powerful full-text search engine so you can find exactly the solution you need.

Printer-friendly!
Print articles for a bound archive and quick desk reference.

Working Sample Code Solutions!
Many articles include complete downloadable sample code ready to adapt for your own projects.

ASPToday covers a broad range of topics including:

- ▶ ASP.NET 1.x and 2.0
- ▶ ADO.NET and SQL
- ▶ XML
- ▶ Web Services
- ▶ E-Commerce

- ▶ Security
- ▶ Site Design
- ▶ Site Admin
- ▶ SMTP and Mail
- ▶ Classic ASP and ADO

and much, much more…

To receive a FREE two-month subscription to ASPToday, visit
www.asptoday.com/subscribe.aspx and answer the question about this book!

forums.apress.com

JOIN THE APRESS FORUMS AND BE PART OF OUR COMMUNITY. You'll find discussions that cover topics of interest to IT professionals, programmers, and enthusiasts just like you. If you post a query to one of our forums, you can expect that some of the best minds in the business—especially Apress authors, who all write with *The Expert's Voice*™—will chime in to help you. Why not aim to become one of our most valuable participants (MVPs) and win cool stuff? Here's a sampling of what you'll find:

DATABASES

Data drives everything.

Share information, exchange ideas, and discuss any database programming or administration issues.

INTERNET TECHNOLOGIES AND NETWORKING

Try living without plumbing (and eventually IPv6).

Talk about networking topics including protocols, design, administration, wireless, wired, storage, backup, certifications, trends, and new technologies.

JAVA

We've come a long way from the old Oak tree.

Hang out and discuss Java in whatever flavor you choose: J2SE, J2EE, J2ME, Jakarta, and so on.

MAC OS X

All about the Zen of OS X.

OS X is both the present and the future for Mac apps. Make suggestions, offer up ideas, or boast about your new hardware.

OPEN SOURCE

Source code is good; understanding (open) source is better.

Discuss open source technologies and related topics such as PHP, MySQL, Linux, Perl, Apache, Python, and more.

PROGRAMMING/BUSINESS

Unfortunately, it is.

Talk about the Apress line of books that cover software methodology, best practices, and how programmers interact with the "suits."

WEB DEVELOPMENT/DESIGN

Ugly doesn't cut it anymore, and CGI is absurd.

Help is in sight for your site. Find design solutions for your projects and get ideas for building an interactive Web site.

SECURITY

Lots of bad guys out there—the good guys need help.

Discuss computer and network security issues here. Just don't let anyone else know the answers!

TECHNOLOGY IN ACTION

Cool things. Fun things.

It's after hours. It's time to play. Whether you're into LEGO® MINDSTORMS™ or turning an old PC into a DVR, this is where technology turns into fun.

WINDOWS

No defenestration here.

Ask questions about all aspects of Windows programming, get help on Microsoft technologies covered in Apress books, or provide feedback on any Apress Windows book.

HOW TO PARTICIPATE:

Go to the Apress Forums site at **http://forums.apress.com/**.
Click the New User link.